STEWART, TABORI & CHANG / NEW YORK

GLUE GUN DECOR

How to DRESS UP YOUR HOME—from PILLOWS and CURTAINS
to SOFAS and LAMPSHADES

MARIAN McEVOY | photographs by CHRIS KENDALL

TO THE READER:

Throughout two decades of ardent glue-gun decorating, I have used at least a dozen types of glue guns. Several of them are mentioned and pictured in this book, but there are many others that are perfectly suited for the projects included in the following pages.

Please bear in mind that I am not aware of all the terrific shops and stores in your specific neighborhoods that specialize in craft items. I would appreciate it if you would e-mail me your best sources for glue-gun decorating materials, glue-gun short cuts, techniques, or any other tips and secrets that can make glue-gun decorating easier and more beautiful. Also, let me know if you need further details on any of the items shown in this book. Share your information, thoughts, and project updates to me at: marian.mcevoy2@verizon.net. I'll get back to you!

Project editor: Sandra Gilbert
Production director: Kim Tyner

Published in 2005 by
Stewart, Tabori & Chang
115 West 18th Street
New York, NY 10011
www.abramsbooks.com

Canadian Distribution:
Canadian Manda Group
One Atlantic Avenue, Suite 105
Toronto, Ontario M6K 3E7
Canada

Library of Congress Cataloging-in-Publication Data

McEvoy, Marian.
    Glue gun decor : how to dress up your home—from pillows and curtains
    to sofas and lampshades / Marian McEvoy ; photographs by Chris Kendall.
        p. cm.
    ISBN 1-58479-416-X
    1. Handicraft. 2. Gluing. 3. House furnishings. 4. Interior decoration—
    Amateurs' manuals. I. Title.

TT157.M4458 2005
745.5—dc22   2004059184

Designed by goodesignny.com
The text of this book was composed in Futura and Clarendon.

Printed in China
10 9 8 7 6 5 4 3 2 1

First Printing

Stewart, Tabori & Chang is a subsidiary of

(first page) A close-up view of a flocked velvet cherry and leaf medallion glue gunned to the back of a simple white sofa.

CONTENTS

ACKNOWLEDGMENTS

Thanks so much to all of you dedicated crafters and do-it-yourself decorators who have shared such original ideas and sure fire tips. Thanks also to my friends at eBay, Sandy Gilbert at Stewart, Tabori & Chang, Joseph Montebello, Kathryn Hammill, and Diane Shaw. To Madison Cox, Alex Reese, Steve and Janine, Ben Brantley, Cynthia Kling, Wayne Lawson, David Colman, Miguel and Nathan, and Billy Sullivan, a giant, sizzling thank you for helping me stick 'em up.

My new guest room celebrates the paisley theme: The burlap curtains are bordered with cut-out Indian paisley motifs; the settee is skirted with a band of printed cotton; and the pillows are festooned with more cutouts. Everything in this picture has been assembled with a glue gun.

GETTING STARTED

It's the best tool I've ever used. Versatile, transportable, easy to operate, and cheaper and lighter than a staple gun or a sewing machine, the hot glue gun has been my number-one decorative ally for over fifteen years. In fact, there's very little in my day-to-day life that hasn't been shot by a glue gun: I sit on glue-gunned cushions, peek through glue-gunned curtains, sleep under a glue-gunned bedspread, serve cocktails on a glue-gunned tray, apply makeup in front of a glue-gunned mirror, read under a glue-gunned lampshade, and am currently typing this sentence on top of a glue-gunned table.

This neo-gothic chair, lampshade, jewelry box, and pair of curtains were all dolled up with the help of a glue gun. I added narrow black braided cord to the edges and seams of the lampshade; applied striped grosgrain ribbon and feathers to the cardboard box; attached wide black moire' ribbon to the curtains' edges; and adhered a geometric-shaped Moroccan embroidery to the seat back.

AFTER PERMANENTLY APPLYING THOUSANDS OF ELEMENTS TO THOUSANDS OF SURFACES, I've learned that decorating with a hot glue gun is the ultimate exercise in instant gratification. Armed with a steady aim, pretty good hand-eye coordination, a strong trigger finger, a stronger pair of reading glasses, and a tolerance for the occasional minor burn that will occur, my addiction to glue gunning gets more intense with every project. From stretching industrial-strength bubble wrap over drafty windows to completely re-covering and reupholstering a nineteenth-century French daybed, my glue-gun projects have been as swiftly accomplished as they are amazingly affordable. Why wait months (and pay gobs of money) for an upholsterer to re-cover a wing chair when I can do it myself for a dime and in a day? What's the point of shelling out five hundred dollars for a so-so seamstress to hem and trim two pairs of curtains when I can handle it for about ten dollars? (Or, for that matter, how could I rationalize dragging out the sewing machine, oiling it up, finding and rewinding the bobbins, and making a trek to the fabric shop to find the right color thread when I can shoot those curtains up in about seventy-five minutes?) And, finally, why do I have to replace my faded but beloved, perfectly sized and shaped pillows or lampshades when I can refurbish them to make them like new?

I rigged up this red and white dining room for the first eBay showhouse. Using furniture, fixtures, art, fabric, and materials found exclusively on eBay, I combined shopping online with glue-gun decorating, something that I do almost every week of my life! The six French dining chairs were reupholstered and then adorned with embroidered flowers.

The walls were covered with red cotton duck fabric and wide black grosgrain ribbon trim. The white muslin curtain panels were decorated with embroidered motifs. All these design elements were applied with a glue gun. Even the drawings, prints, and watercolors were rematted and reframed thanks to a hot glue gun.

GLUE-GUN MAKERS RACKED UP NEARLY TEN MILLION DOLLARS IN SALES LAST YEAR. Thousands of glue guns are used by part-time crafters, but an equal number are owned by full-time construction workers and even hairdressers. There are low-heat, two-inch-long "mini" guns for attaching dollhouse shingles to dollhouse roofs; there are scorching-hot, two-foot-long industrial glue guns for melding airport walls to airport floors; and there are literally hundreds of different models of glue guns that are just the right size (about six inches long) and strength (both low- and high-heat options) for do-it-yourself interior decorators like me. (As for which types many hair stylists wield to attach hair extensions, I think I'll just stick with the "don't ask, don't tell" approach.)

Perhaps the most prolific—and most clever—glue gunners of all are the thousands of florists and wedding party planners who rely on hot glue for quick, temporary decorative fixes. These time- and budget-pressed professionals use glue guns to apply moss to flower-pots, place branches and vines on and around tent poles, ground centerpieces on tables, and secure flowers to stems. I learned a lot of tips and tricks through watching and questioning party planners in action, but this book is not about projects or effects that last for only one night. *Glue Gun Decor* is about creating permanent designs. And although I know lots of crafty people use glue guns for making repairs (reconstituting broken pottery, anchoring tiles to floors, reattaching knobs to cabinets, and securing loose soles to shoes), this book will not show you how to fix anything broken. It will help you make something beautiful. More precisely, it'll show you how to turn decorative ducks into swans.

My living room was bright, sunny, and roomy enough for lots of people, so it was no surprise when somebody eventually spilled a glass of red wine all over the seat of this formerly all-white sofa. Never one to mourn over ruined upholstery, I re-covered the stained white cushion by glue gunning it over with an old red wool shawl. Then I found a big box full of flocked motifs featuring cherries and leaves that I had cut out of a pair of old curtains. I arranged them in a medallion pattern on the back of the sofa and then trailed a swath of them up the front of the arms, across the center of the lower front panel, and up the seams that separate the back from the arms.

I liked the cheery cherry motif so much that I added them to the top of a plain beige upholstered footstool to match.

STYLE NOTE: The white-painted doors, ceiling, and moldings throughout the room give a sense of space, calm, and neatness.

IF YOU CRAVE PERSONALIZED, UNIQUELY EMBEL-
LISHED FURNITURE, DECORATIVE ACCESSORIES, AND
WALLS, THIS BOOK CAN HELP MAKE THEM HAPPEN.
I'll show you that a session with a hot glue gun can
transform a ho-hum chair seat into a showpiece or adhere
a fancy pleated skirt to a wallflower dressing table or
energize a plain lampshade with bright trim or make an
inexpensive picture frame into a one-of-a-kind treasure.

Like knitting or needlepoint, decorative glue gunning
is calming and cathartic: Many repetitive steps and ges-
tures can add up to one big effect. But unlike needlecrafts,
glue-gunning techniques are minimal. There are no fancy
stitches to master and no complicated attachments to
grapple with. Once you get the hang of dispensing and
applying an even, steady stream of the scorching-hot,
sticky substance that dries very quickly, there's nothing
you can't adhere to almost any surface in your home. From
upholstering headboards to placing braided trims or
embroidered motifs on lampshades, curtains, and pillows to
encrusting entire walls with designs made up of bunches of
natural elements like seeds or shells, glue gunning is not
only a craft, but also a miraculous means of transformation.

(opposite) This parrot green entry hall came alive when I added a little black and white Egyptian revival table, two of my white dining chairs, and a cherry-colored woven plastic mat. The glue-gunned items? The fabric-covered cushions; the rickrack-embellished lampshade, and the decorative prints that are glue gunned into their frames.

(above) Glue-gunned upholstery holds up under duress. This is one of a pair of Eastlake chairs that I found at a Laguna Beach antique fair. When I bought them, they were meticulously upholstered in pristine plain white cotton, but years of use resulted in stains, smudges, and spots on both the seat and the back. With the aid of a glue gun, I re-covered the chair backs and seats with a layer of crisp sandy beige linen, an easy fabric to work with because it has lots of give and stretch. After the fabric was on good and tight, I cut out and applied several embroidered circular motifs from a large Suzani cloth I found on eBay. To finish it off, I glue gunned a stripe of red elastic trim to all the borders. The upholstery on the daybed was also glue gunned. So was the slim black trim on the lampshade.

15

I DISCOVERED THE MYRIAD APPLICATIONS AND CHARMS OF GLUE GUNNING WHEN I DECIDED TO CAMOUFLAGE ONE OF MY TWO GIGANTIC, BUT REALLY UGLY, FIREPLACES WITH A LAYER OF HUNDREDS OF DENSELY PACKED SEASHELLS. I'd gone through a frustrating process of trying to adhere conch and scallop shells to the fireplace's rough, stuccoed surface by using what must have been a gallon of Krazy Glue. The heavier shells fell off, my fingers got stuck together, and the price of those hundreds of little tubes of glue was ridiculous. I was ready to toss everything back into the ocean when an artist friend suggested I try a hot glue gun. I ran out to my local hardware store, bought the first glue gun I saw, plugged it in, loaded it, aimed, fired, and never looked back. Hopefully you, too, will discover glue-gun decorating through this book. Whatever the motivation, glue gunning is a decorating adventure that evolves and advances as you do. Like so many other skills that we develop in our lives, the more you do it, the better you get. Practice might not make perfect, but it sure improves the performance. Let's go!

It all started here: This huge fireplace was the first decorative project I attacked with a glue gun. Without the shells and paint, it was an unfortunate combination of white stucco and faded, dirty red bricks. It looked heavy, clunky, and—at a whopping ten feet across— too big for its own good. I needed to give it some charm and to personalize it.

STEP ONE: First, I cleaned the brick and stucco by brushing it with a mild detergent and wiping it dry with old towels. I then painted both the brick and stucco with two coats of black matte acrylic interior paint. I allowed a full day for each coat to dry, as the surface was extremely uneven and porous.

STEP TWO: I love the sharp graphic impact of black and white, so I decided that all-white shells would be the perfect accent for the black fireplace. I gathered up about six hundred shells of varying sizes and shapes and painted them front, sides, and back. Again, I allowed one day of drying time for each coat of paint, as shells are porous and jagged.

STEP THREE: I then divided the shells into eight piles of distinct types and species: from small to medium to pointed to spiraled to fluted. I put each shell type into a separate basket arranged on one large tray. Starting from the inside of the fireplace, I glued straight lines of similar shells in "concentric" patterns radiating outward, apply- ing glue along the entire length of each shell to ensure maximum adhesion. The trick is to make your shell patterns repetitive and not random. A helter-skelter approach produces a messy, decidedly nongraphic look. You want a well- planned effect. On the outer sides of the fireplace, I loosened up the striped graphic approach by design- ing two round shell medallions in the center of each vertical space. To add dimension and surprise, I glued shells vertically along the top edge of the mantel so that they stood up on the surface.

STEP FOUR: The crowning glory was the shelled mirror. My friend, decorator Muriel Brandolini, found this beauty for me in Paris, where it was glue gunned by a gifted French artisan. This shelled fireplace stayed in great shape for over eight years. Every other month or so, when the fireplace was not in use, I cleaned the shells with a long- bristled, soft brush spritzed with a bit of alcohol and detergent. A note of caution: Do not glue shells too close to areas where flames flicker. The shells won't combust, but they will fall off if the glue is loosened and reactivated by too much heat.

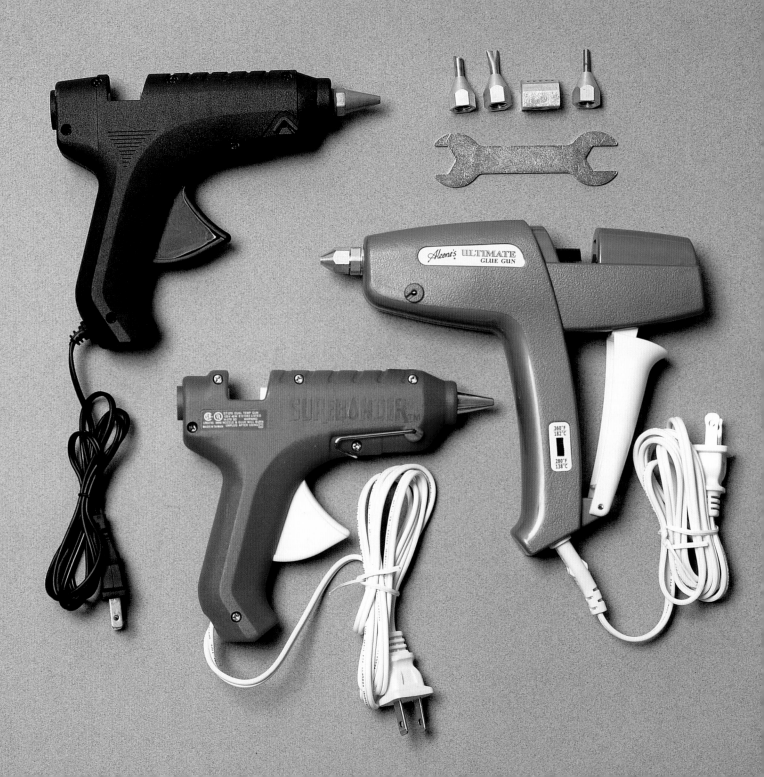

1 | TOOLS YOU NEED

There are dozens of glue guns on the market. The glue gun you need for decorating is a craft (not a construction) model. From three to eight inches in length, made of lightweight, durable plastic, all glue guns are designed to accept only one size of glue stick, ranging from an eighth to three eighths of an inch in diameter. My favorite model and brand is the gold one pictured here — Aleene's Ultimate Glue Gun. It has a large, easy-to-squeeze handle/trigger, a switch to change glue flow and temperature and a collection of four different nozzles, plus a small wrench to help screw them on.

The cords on most glue guns are about four feet long, so you need to add an extension cord to enable you to move freely around your work area. Most glue guns take about five minutes to warm up. If you start squeezing the trigger before the gun is fired up, the glue will be too hard and rubbery to adhere to any surface.

Glue-gun decorating goes smoothly and quickly if you have a design plan and if your equipment is organized. If you have all your tools, gadgets, materials, and aids rounded up and arranged within reach, your glue-gunning sessions will be more successful and a lot more fun. Jumping up every five minutes to grab something that you forgot is a frustrating waste of time. I keep the twenty or so tools and items I use for glue gunning in a large, hard-sided suitcase that I carry from room to room, from project to project. When I am ready to work, I open the suitcase, take out the items I need, and line them up on a large wooden tray placed right next to whatever table or flat surface I am working on.

FOR MOST DECORATIVE GLUE-GUN GOALS—INCLUDING TRIMMING LAMPSHADES AND PILLOWS, EMBELLISHING CURTAINS, COVERING WALLS, AND RE-COVERING FURNITURE—YOU WILL NEED THE FOLLOWING ARTILLERY: FIRST AND FOREMOST, A RELIABLE GLUE GUN. A, trusty, four-star glue gun is one that doesn't leak. Glue-gun leak occurs without warning and sometimes continues nonstop. When a hot glue stick is inserted into the gun's cylindrical heating chamber along the top of the gun, the resulting clear, syrupy liquid exits the nozzle as you press the trigger. Unfortunately, the liquid glue can also drizzle out when you aren't applying pressure, creating a mess that's a nightmare to clean up. Leaky glue guns are also the cause of painful burns that can occur when glue unexpectedly seeps out of glue gun nozzles. After using about thirty different brands and models, I've found very few glue guns that don't develop a leak problem after about a week's worth of use. Not surprisingly, the cheaper a glue gun is, the more it leaks. If you think that $7.99 budget gun at your local craft supply shop is a great deal, think again. Add on an extra twenty dollars or so and get yourself a tool that will give you professional results.

The best gun in the business is a bronzy-gold model called Aleene's Ultimate Glue Gun. It is carried by many sewing and fabric shops, and most neighborhood and national crafts store chains. At less than thirty dollars, this is a honey of a tool. It weighs about two pounds, is about seven inches long, and includes a switch that let's you regulate heat and flow, from low and thick ("Regular") to high and thin ("Super Flow"). It comes in a small carrying case that houses four different nozzles. One is cone-shaped with an opening the size of a small peppercorn, and one is about an eighth of an inch wide, with a tip pressed flat and almost closed, but I find that the most efficient of the group is the half-inch-long cylinder with the end cut off at an angle. This slim slanted nozzle emits an ideally sized stream of glue (about a sixteenth of an inch wide), which is perfect for working with intricate embroidered motifs and narrow strips of ribbon and trim. It allows you to get close in and under the piece you are gluing down. The second most useful nozzle is a thick metal wedge seven-eighths of an inch long, with tiny holes running the length of the wedge. This clever attachment is great for applying wide ribbons or trims to walls, paper, or fabric. It emits a solid, flat trail of hot glue that is about six times wider than that made by a pointed nozzle. It anchors your trim or ribbon from edge to edge. The attachments can be easily screwed on the tip of Aleene's Ultimate Glue Gun when it is warm (not hot) so that you can switch from wider to narrower nozzles as you are working.

You can't have enough glue sticks. There's nothing more maddening than interrupting a merry glue-gunning rhythm because you've run out of supplies. For most projects, the long, supple twelve-inch sticks bought in craft stores are miles better than the shorter six-inch versions sold by large hardware chains. And the twelve-inchers are cheap as well! During sales, snap up a hundred of them. The smaller, packaged glue sticks that you find in hardware stores are about six times as expensive and of no better quality.

You'll have to search further for washable glue sticks: Craft stores carry them, but I've noticed that supplies dwindle quickly. Again, when you find them, buy enough for a couple of months. Finally, there are lots of new inventive twists in the glue stick world, but I find that the new glittered, fluorescent, and wildly colored hot glue sticks don't suit my kind of decorating. I don't need—or want—my glue to be visible. It's a means to an end, not the end.

TIP: A glue-gun appendage that drives me nuts is the little folding metal "stand" attached near the nozzles of all glue guns. Manufacturers tell you to "always prop your gun up" on these flimsy little gizmos, but I find that struggling to balance a gun on a spindly folding structure is a waste of time. I remove the stand and place the glue side on a foot-square piece of ceramic tile. If glue does leak, I can peel it off the tile in a heartbeat. It is also easier to grab the gun when it is lying on its side.

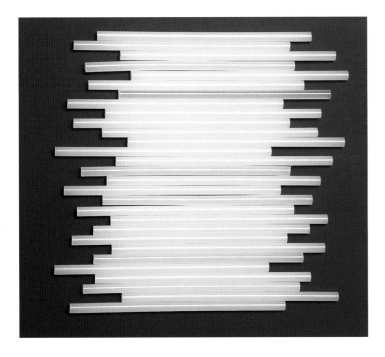

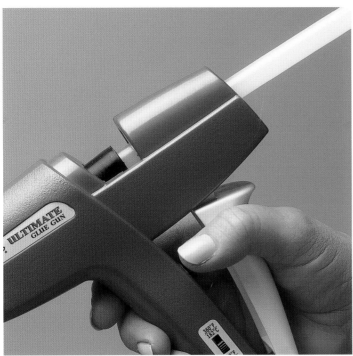

GLUE-GUN MAINTENANCE IS EASY AND SWIFT: ALWAYS UNPLUG THE GLUE GUN WHEN IT IS NOT IN USE. Before the gun gets completely cold, rub it down with a soft dishcloth moistened with warm water and a few drops of rubbing alcohol, which will help remove any residual glue on the nozzle or handle.

Once you've got your reliable gun, you'll need a twenty-foot extension cord for mobility when working on large-scale projects, including applying designs to a wall and re-covering or embellishing large pieces of furniture. For all glued decorating projects except tiny touch-ups, the twelve-inch-long glue sticks sold at crafts stores are more practical than the six-inch models sold at hardware stores. The fewer times you have to reload your glue gun, the faster and more consistent your results.

Before you start glue-gun decorating, you will need to practice your hot-glue technique. You must learn to get your elements in place, insert the glue in between the "host" surface and the "add-on" items, and then apply light pressure with your fingertips before the hot glue cools and hardens. Some glue-gun manufacturers contend that you have up to three minutes before the hot, syrupy glue dries and turns to the consistency of a rubber band, but you've actually got a lot less. I've found that most hot glues set fairly firmly in less than ten seconds, so working quickly is a must. Keep in mind that glue gunning in cold temperatures is more difficult than during a heat wave. My upstate New York house is startlingly chilly during winter, and I've noticed that searingly hot glue hardens and sets about twice as quickly in January as in August. On a hot, humid day, glue can take up to a minute to set. Weather matters!

NO MATTER HOW ADEPT YOU ARE AT GLUE GUNNING, YOU CANNOT AVOID GLUE-GUN "STRINGS." These tiny spiderweb-like filaments are produced when you draw the glue gun away from the surface you are working on. You might also be plagued by the random drips and smears that happen when your hand shifts or when the glue misses, or overreaches, its target. To get rid of these strings, wait until the glue is dry and cool and then use a soft-bristle toothbrush to gather the strings together and remove them. Unwanted globs and drops are tougher to eradicate, particularly if they are stuck to the porous surfaces of most fabrics, stucco, and paper. Again, wait until the glue is thoroughly cool and set. Use a wooden toothpick, a pair of tweezers, or a fingernail to pick, pluck, and lift the drop from the surface. If you've got a stubborn, messy glue smear, try rubbing the surface and the surrounding area with a cloth lightly dampened with rubbing alcohol, and then pry it off. Sometimes the smear is just too stubborn to lift off: As a last resort, find a felt-tip pen in the same color as the surface material and draw over the glue mark.

When working with pieces of cut-out appliqués, crewelwork, or embroidery, remember that the edges will most likely fray if you do not "seal" them first. (The threads in most woven cotton or silk fabrics loosen and unravel when cut.) Aleene comes to the rescue again with a product designed to eliminate messy trailing threads and edges. Keep several bottles of Aleene's Stop Fraying glue in your supply kit. It works on wool, knitted braid trim, ribbon edges, and just about any fabric pieces you might use. Take a slim, natural-bristle paintbrush, dip it in a dab of Aleene's Stop Fraying, and paint the edges of all cut fabrics with a thin coat of glue. If you apply too much, your edges will look as though they are embalmed in a clunky plastic ridge, something to be avoided. Stop Fraying goes on bluish-white, dries almost clear, and takes about fifteen minutes to set, so be sure to allow enough time between fray gluing and hot gluing your pieces down. For items that need to be laundered, you must use Aleene's Fabric Glue Sticks.

Scissors can make the difference between a polished looking project and an amateur mess. Quality is crucial. An inferior pair of manicure scissors—or a cheap pair of shears—won't cut it. Bypass those cheap plastic and aluminum scissors in the supermarket and go for the stainless steel ones used by hairdressers, tailors, and manicurists. A pair of scissors made by Wüsthof, Henckels, DOVO, André Tisserand, Jaguar, Messermeister, Rubis, or Janome is better than anything you can pick up at a drugstore or dollar shop.

Glue-gun decorating is a fun but exacting process. You must concentrate, establish a comfortable work pace, hone your focus, and pay attention to details. These are some tools that will help you perfect your craft.

If your decorative glue gunning entails working with fabrics, silk lampshades, cushions, and pillows, the most important tool in your arsenal is a panoply of good-quality scissors. I always keep about five or six pairs, in five or six different sizes, lined up immediately to the right of the surface I am working on. My basic set includes tiny curved cuticle scissors for snipping around scalloped edges and corners, a snub-nosed pair for working on loosely woven materials, embroidery clippers, and seven-inch-long shears for cutting lengths of cotton. For edging and trimming in tight, difficult spots, a pointed, razor-sharp mat knife will also work.

Other tools that help glue-gun decorating go swimmingly are a small natural-bristle paintbrush for applying Aleene's Stop Fraying glue, a graphite pencil for tracing shapes and designs, a soft-bristle toothbrush and a makeup brush for whisking away glue strings and errant threads, and a pair of first-rate tweezers for plucking away stubborn glue drips and other particles.

TIP: If you don't live near a high quality knife or sewing shop, you can buy top-tier scissors online.

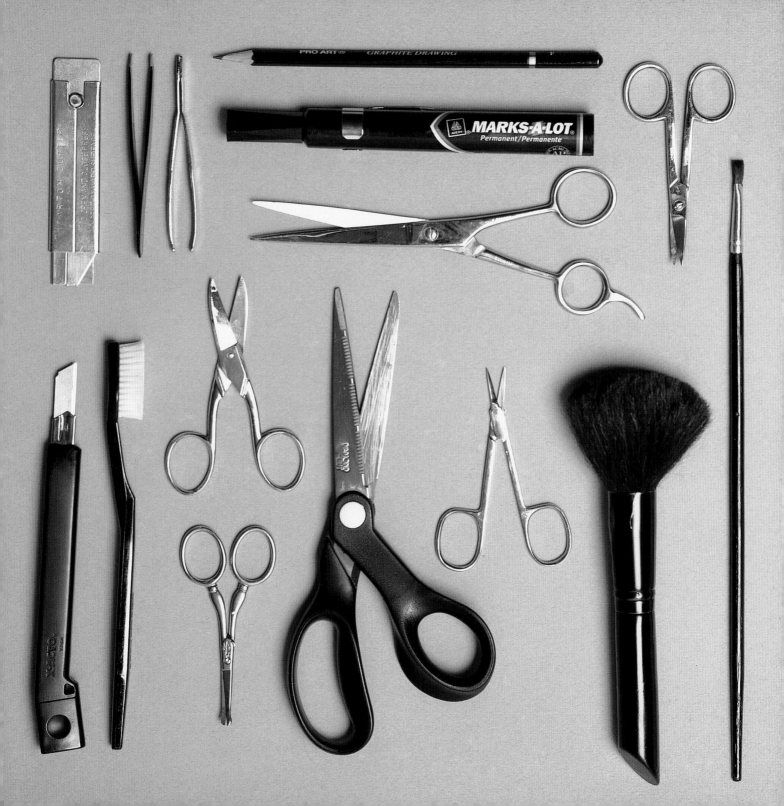

IF YOUR SCISSORS DO NOT HAVE TIGHT CONTACTS BETWEEN THE BLADES, YOU WILL WASTE TIME TRYING TO GET CLEAN EDGES. A very sharp, pointed mat knife is also necessary to get into hard–to-reach places with hanging thread problems. If you are reupholstering or covering a chair, you will need to cut excess fabric away often; a pair of salon-quality haircutting scissors will do the job nicely.

Cloth measuring tapes work better than metal ones for most glue-gun decorating projects. Measuring materials for curtains or sizing pieces of fabric for seat cushions and sofa arms and backs involves the sort of curves and hilly terrains best handled by a supple cloth tape that gives a more accurate measure than a stiff one.

A graphite pencil and a soft rubber eraser will also help you reach your glue-gunning goals. Before gluing your items to the "host surface," mark the spot with a pencil outline. When affixing leaves to a square canvas, for example, position the leaf where you want it and draw a faint pencil line around the curves. If the host surface is dark, use white tailor's chalk to make marks. If you are designing a mural, always start your art in the center of the wall. If your designs are grounded in the center of the space, the little placement mistakes you might make at the top, bottom, left, and right will be less noticeable.

When you work on curtain panels, bed covers, seat cushions, pillows, silk lampshades, or any other soft material surface, pin the trims and motifs into place. Sewing pins with round colored balls at the ends are easier to see and better to work with than plain straight pins. Do not buy the cheap versions, though; the balls pull off easily. Ask for Singer brand ball-topped pins. They're stronger, thicker, and they last longer. To glue items pinned to a surface, remove one pin at a time and place a small amount of glue under the pinned area. Continue in this way, removing pins as you go.

Try to establish a rhythm as you work. Do not attempt to glue down too large an area at once. For example, if you are putting a narrow grosgrain ribbon around the edges of a picture frame, glue down and lightly secure no more than two inches of ribbon at a time. When attaching small shells to a box, one shell at a time is as fast as you should go. Remember, hot glue cools down fast, so you've got to press items into place when the glue is still pliant and warm.

Large and heavy objects, such as tiles, squares of mirror, conch shells, or jumbo pinecones should be secured with a generous amount of hot glue placed on every point of contact between the object and its host surface. Do not attach cumbersome or weighty objects with just a bit of hot glue on the top and bottom; they won't stay attached for long.

You'll need two types of measuring tools: a soft cloth tape measure for getting across, around, and under upholstery and pillows, and a stiff, retractable metal tape measure if you plan to work on walls. To help you inspect tiny details, you need both a magnifying glass and a pair of magnifying reading glasses, even if you don't use them for reading. (Eyestrain is a common side effect of glue gunning.)

Aleene's Stop Fraying glue is a miraculous remedy for messy, fraying cut edges on the embroidered and appliquéd motifs you will use to pretty up your pillows and curtains. Good-quality pins are as important as pricey shears: Buy the Singer brand ball-topped sewing pins; they're durable and easy to see and to remove. A loosely woven cotton dishcloth is ideal for wiping your gun free of sticky glue filaments, fabric residue, and threads.

And, finally, a design surprise: As I re-cover, reupholster, and embellish lots of ebonized and black-painted wood furniture, dings, nicks, and scrapes are a constant bother. Before I start re-covering or adding decorative embroidery to these beautiful pieces, I apply a thin coat of Kiwi black liquid shoe polish to all nicked or scratched areas. The polish, which can be applied either with the attached sponge or with a paintbrush, is watery-thin and dries quickly. It's the best furniture cover-up I've ever used.

IN ADDITION TO A SOFT-BRISTLE TOOTHBRUSH, YOU CAN ALSO USE A BIG, FLUFFY MAKEUP BRUSH TO REMOVE GLUE THREADS OR DUST FROM THE PRICKLY SURFACES OF SHELLS, THISTLES, SEEDS, PINECONES, AND PLUSH FABRICS SUCH AS VELVET AND CASHMERE. The gentle bristles of the makeup brush will remove filaments and residue from fragile elements without breaking them. For dry, dusty buildups on any glue-gunned surface, moisten a clean makeup brush with a little soapy water and sweep away. Now that I am over fifty, reading glasses are a part of my everyday life, but even at thirty-five, I wore a pair of light magnifying reading glasses whenever I glue gunned. If, like me, you'll be gluing for hours at a time, it can put a real strain on those super-focused eyes. And be sure you have good light— really seeing what you are doing is half the battle.

If you plan to glue items to your ceiling, a solid ladder is not the only helper you'll need: You must wear protective eye goggles because hot glue drips down. You might also consider wearing a hat or scarf over your hair. I can't tell you how many times I got down from a ladder with my long bob clotted in drops and globs of glue. Talk about a bad hair day.

A few more things to remember: Dried glue can generally be peeled off hard nonporous surfaces. But the crafter who has smeared a drip of hot glue on fabric, untreated wood, paper, suede, or stucco will have a pretty tough time getting rid of it. Peeling dried glue off an old painted surface will remove the paint and most likely the plaster underneath. On many fabrics, a hot glue smear is permanent. So aim carefully, work in small increments, apply light pressure to the trigger, and if a big drop of searing glue still lands where you don't want it, wait until it is completely dry and cool before you try to pluck it off.

Neat, tailored glue-gun decorating involves outlining all kinds of objects, accessories, and furniture with a border of braid or ribbon.

Don't settle for the expected, classic braided wool or silk passementerie trims. Finish off your pillows, picture frames, and curtains with surprising, imaginative materials. Why not edge a dining chair seat cushion with grosgrain ribbon made for clothing? What about using industrial cotton webbed tape to cover the top and bottom edges of a lampshade? How about adding a line of brightly colored macramé cord to the outer edge of a wooden mirror frame?

Among my ever-growing collection of trims, my favorites are a dozen huge reels of braided acrylic macramé yarns; shiny plastic lanyard strips; antique moiré and flocked velvet ribbons; thick, wide cotton tape used for finishing off mattresses; and, my happiest discovery of all, yards of narrow, ribbed elastic in eighteen different colors. I've found that trimming almost anything with elastic is better than using thin-skinned ribbon: It is thick, and you can pull, twist, and tease a border of elastic trim into almost any shape.

I have found many yards of one-of-a-kind vintage trims at auctions and swap meets, but the biggest supplier by far of my trim wardrobe is eBay.

Check out the diminutive one-tenth-inch-wide powder blue elastic with a tiny lacy edge. Or the one-and-a-half-inch bright red ribbed elastic with one shiny side and one matte. I go through about thirty yards of half-inch black elastic every month to spruce up the sofa cushions and pillows that I use in my house and give away as gifts.

TIP: Do not scratch or rub at an area with a smeared glue mistake; you'll just make it worse.

WHATEVER MATERIALS YOU CHOOSE FOR YOUR EMBELLISHMENT PROJECTS, BUY OR GATHER UP PLENTY OF THEM, BECAUSE YOU WILL ALWAYS END UP USING MORE THAN YOU ANTICIPATE. I keep an arsenal of ribbon, elastic, and braid trims in a dozen different colors on hand at all glue-gun moments. And because I also bond copious quantities of dried leaves, shells, acorns, seeds, and pinecones to many surfaces, I stockpile these items as well. There's nothing worse than designing a pair of dried-leaf pictures and then running out of leaves. You won't be able to collect more of them until the next fall, so grab a couple thousand of them when they're lying around.

Glue-gun decorating is not simply a matter of sticking things together; it's a process of permanently attaching beautiful items to beautiful surfaces—and you'll want a big choice of both. Even if you think you will never use the appliquéd motifs on that beautiful old, stained tablecloth or the vintage beads on that hand-me-down evening top, or those extraordinarily colored maple leaves that cover your lawn in October, grab them, keep them, and discover them again for a future project.

Nature lovers, unite! There are few pastimes that please me more than affixing natural elements to fireplace mantels, ceilings, walls, and moldings. In a seaside home, a shell-encrusted bathroom, bedroom, or hall is a fun project in which children and friends can participate. In the country or the mountains, pinecones, acorns, and dried thistles and weeds can look ravishing placed strategically on a wall or in a picture frame.

A few of the items that I've used to cover various flat surfaces, clockwise from top left: turkey feathers, medium-sized pinecones, wheat shafts, large pale pinecones, dried thistles, and round pods. The trick to preserving your designs is to make sure the "bits of nature" are completely dry before you glue them. Brush them off before you glue to remove any bits of dirt, dust, or shriveled leaves or stems. Apply the glue to each contact point so that they stay in place.

Embellishing pillows is the simplest, most immediately satisfying glue-gunning project you can tackle. Every home can benefit from a select battery of smart, decorative cushions strewn across sofa backs, tucked into window seat corners, propped on arm chairs, fluffed up on beds, and stacked helter-skelter in kids' rooms. With a dozen or so pillows, you can show off your creative glue-gunned labors in almost every room in the house. A nicely detailed pillow is a terrific gift, too. Last Christmas, I gave twenty friends and relatives one-of-a-kind glue-gunned pillows jazzed up with various bits of antique embroidery. They've all asked for more.

The flower adorned pillows and glue-gunned trim lampshade help pull this living room together.

This sofa is beautifully made, so I didn't want to do too much to it. I did want to personalize it and make it look a bit less large and bare, though, so I glue gunned red and black braided wool trim up the front of the arms and over the seams between the back of the sofa and the arms. A glue gun was also used to decorate the flower-encrusted pillows and the braid-trimmed lampshade. A finishing touch: a plain round cardboard box from the local craft shop got the gun treatment with bands of striped ribbon, a perky bow, and a few feathers on the top. The red throw over the sofa is an old cashmere shawl whose ends had become too frayed to wear.

THE SECRET TO CHIC PILLOW DESIGN IS TO START WITH AN UNADORNED, NONTUFTED, SOLID-COLORED SQUARE OR BOLSTER SHAPE. Top-of-the-line pillows are stuffed with down, goose feathers, or natural cotton fibers and batting, but if you find a synthetic stuffing that doesn't feel like Styrofoam or rubbery cotton candy, go for it. Pillows upholstered in busy prints or shiny damasks—or trimmed in sparkly beaded fringe or tassels—are not good candidates for the projects in this chapter. Buy something basic: A neutral, solid-colored pillow sheathed in a natural fabric is like a clean piece of white drawing paper—it's ready for whatever you want to add to it. Plain pillows are available at all price points in all types of stores, but if you want to decorate more than a few, it makes sense to shop for bargains on the Web, and at all types of stores—from discount to top-of-the-line. When you find a good plain pillow, do buy it in bulk.

(left) A baker's dozen of some of the glue-gunned pillows that accessorize my house: All of them started out life as solid-colored citizens. Most are embellished with cut-out embroidery from a dozen or so cloths from Uzbekistan, but several of them are souped up with homemade red tassels made from unraveled macramé cord.

(above) Here's a good plain shot of a good plain pillow. The good news: It is the perfect blank canvas for glue-gun decorating because the fringe is not too fancy, and the fabric is 100 percent raw silk. The bad news: It is stuffed with bouncy, resistant synthetic fibers that make it feel a bit like a soft basketball. But at four dollars a pop, I can learn to live with synthetic.

BEFORE BEGINNING A PROJECT LIKE THIS, ORGANIZE YOUR WORKSPACE. Clear off a desk or dining table and cover it with a painter's drop cloth or kraft paper. If you're over five feet tall, after an hour or so of glue gunning your back might start complaining, so rig up a desk or dining chair with several cushions to raise you over the table. Make sure your extension cord is long enough to accommodate all your movements and positions. Start your pillow embellishment by attaching trim to all four sides.

Use Aleene's long slanted nozzle attachment and squeeze the hot glue out in a uniform thin stream. Work in two-inch increments, first applying glue to the ribbon or elastic, then laying the trim into place on the pillow, then pressing the ribbon down with your fingers for several seconds until the glue cools. After the trim is glued down, the real "decorating" begins. I keep an arsenal of embroidered floral patterns, geometric motifs, and meandering leaf and vine designs cut out from vintage curtain panels, shawls, tablecloths, and Suzani textiles, snapped up at local

auctions, yard sales, and on eBay, so that I can adorn pillows and lampshades whenever the mood strikes. The larger your choice, the better the results. Suzanis are constructed of homespun cotton and embroidered silk. They were traditionally made for wedding dowries by tribal women in Uzbekistan. Most of the Suzanis today are done by machine; they're less sophisticated and poetic than antique examples, but they are still cheerful and highly decorative. Four or five women typically work on one cloth for months, sometimes years, before it is completed.

(opposite) This is an excellent example of the vintage Suzani textiles that I find on eBay. This 1940s beauty is faded and frayed in spots, which is what I prefer. If a textile is too perfect, it seems a shame to cut it up. Measuring about four by six feet, the ninety-dollar price seemed like a real bargain. When it arrived, I cut out the six circular forms and placed one each in the center of six twenty-inch square pillows, which are now flanking the back of one of my sofas.

(above) These crewel-embroidered floral, branch, and leaf remnants were extracted from a tablecloth. The intricate designs took three hours to clip away from their host cloth.

35

FOR MEMORABLE PILLOW DESIGN, choose a group of embroideries in different sizes and place them as follows: A nine-inch-wide flower should be placed at the center of a pillow with equal space on all four sides. Smaller embroidered pieces will look better if they are placed in all four corners. Do not try to load up any pillow—no matter how large—with too many disparate designs and colors, or it might have the look of a schizophrenic carnival. Be sure to seal the fraying edges of cut-out embroideries with an application of Aleene's Stop Fraying. Using a small, slim natural-bristle paintbrush, apply a spare amount on all edges of the fabric. Allow fifteen minutes for drying time before you start hot gluing.

When you begin planning your pillow design, pin the components into place. Look at the pillow from several angles and then move the parts around until they feel "at home." The most successful pillow designs are symmetrical: a sixteen-, seventeen-, eighteen-, or twenty-four-inch square looks more powerful if all its sides are treated equally!

If you are glue gunning pillows to accessorize a modern streamlined room, forego flowers and frou frou. Go with a simple tailored border of one or two bands of ribbon or cord applied on all four of the pillow edges. Turn the pillow over and repeat the process again.

At some point in your pillow glue-gunning session, you will be nonplussed by the weblike glue filaments that form each time you draw the glue gun away from the area you're working on. Wait until you are finished gluing and then use a soft-bristle toothbrush to gather the threads together, up, and away.

(above) To ensure sure-fire pillow results, pin your motifs into place with easy-to-see colored ball-topped sewing pins. These bright, cheery flowers, buds, and leaves were cut out of a Suzani textile, and I decided that four of them would look fun and splashy together on one single pillow.

(left) Many glue gun users say that the most maddening aspect of hot glue application is the wispy glue filaments that form whenever a glue gun is moved away from the working surface. The best way to round up and banish stubborn hot glue filaments is by whooshing a soft-bristle toothbrush around, and back and forth, over the area after the hot glue has cooled.

(above) When your embroidered motifs are this large, you need to leave some "air" around them. Placed in the center of the pillow, the fluted-edged circular piece gets some added drama and scale by flanking it with four smaller, contrasting designs.

(left) Applying this little embroidered decorative squiggle was a challenge. The edges are more irregular than the coast of Maine, and the fraying was beyond severe. Although I applied Aleene's Stop Fraying around all edges, lots of little red threads refused to behave. The solution? A pair of eyebrow tweezers. It took ten minutes to extract the threads. The more jagged the edges, the more time it will take you to glue gun your embroidery down.

LAMPSHADES ARE ANOTHER HOUSEHOLD STAPLE THAT CAN BE EASILY CUSTOMIZED AND GLAMORIZED BY A BIT OF ARTFUL HOT GLUE GUNNING. Every room of my house—including the screened-in porch and the powder room—has table lamps or chandeliers topped with shades trimmed expressly for their surroundings. As lampshades are pricey and fragile, you should do plenty of "dress rehearsals" on old shades.

This group shot shows eight great ways to chic up your plain shades.

(clockwise from upper left): A stained tablecloth provided the embroidered flowers and leaves for this red-bordered paper shade; large black rickrack zigzags down and across this red and white lampshade; a pleated plastic shade looks a lot better with the addition of regularly spaced vertical ribbon stripes in periwinkle blue and black; a dressing room shade gets dolled up with a big ochre satin bow and an antique passementerie brooch, and two borders covered in burgundy grosgrain ribbon; I used tiny acorn-shaped embroidered bits to animate a pleated silk shade; this gently curved bedroom lampshade looks more important with a hot pink and black border trim job; a six-faced, black-bordered shade got extra oomph when I added Kelly green grosgrain ribbon trim around each of the six panels; I glue gunned feathers over the stains on this four-sided parchment lampshade and then drew branches with a black felt-tip pen.

(above) These four pristine shades were part of a huge lampshade windfall that I received after the decorator Albert Hadley cleaned out one of his warehouses.

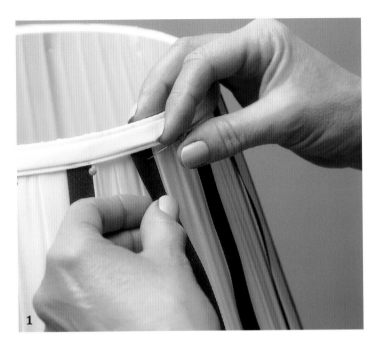

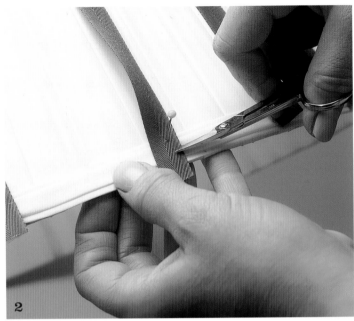

HOW EASILY AND QUICKLY YOUR LAMPSHADE GLUE GUNNING GOES DEPENDS ON WHETHER YOU WILL BE WORKING ON SHADES MADE OF PAPER, PLEATED SILK, PLASTIC, PARCHMENT, STIFF COTTON, METAL, OR RAFFIA. Metal is the most difficult to handle (you can't pin motifs or trim in place), and plastic is a huge challenge because the hot glue warps—and sometimes melts—the plastic you are trying to glue.

As is the case with pillows, the most alluringly transformed lampshades begin with plain, solid-colored backgrounds. No matter how intricate a shade's shape or how densely a shade might be pleated or tucked, a solid color will be a better canvas to work on.

Take a pleated plastic shade from nasty looking to fun and chic in four quick steps.

STEP ONE: If you're considering camouflaging a less than brilliant pleated lampshade, consider placing strips of ribbon in regular vertical stripes around the shade's circumference. First, I pinned pieces of periwinkle blue cotton ribbon in place at regular intervals starting at the top. As the white border was a bit loose, it allowed me to nudge the strips of ribbon underneath, which made for a neater look.

STEP TWO: After each strip was pinned into place at the top of the shade, I cut the bottom off, tucked the edge under the border, and pinned it in place.

CHOOSING A SHADE CAN BE DAUNTING. Some are lined in gold paper so they reflect a warm light; some are intricately sheathed in two layers of pleated silk; some are flimsy paper covers attached to bare-bones metal forms; and some look like metal "coolie" hats. No matter what shade you select, think of it as the spouse of your lamp base: They've got to complement each other because they'll be together for more than a one-night stand. In general, squat bases need similarly chunky shades. Tall, slim bases demand graceful lean shades. A little bedside table lamp looks best with a diminutive shade, and a solid, formidable standing lamp should get topped off with something hefty, tall, and wide. I have found myriad shade sizes and types on eBay, but I have also bought really nice shades at yard sales and charity auctions. (Totally re-covering a lampshade with new fabric or parchment is a huge ordeal that I don't recommend. Buy a new one.)

STEP THREE: Starting from bottom to top, I applied a small amount of hot glue to the ribbon strip and then pressed it into place. Because plastic will wilt and melt when it comes into contact with hot glue, turn your temperature switch to the low "Regular" setting and work quickly.

STEP FOUR: Finally, to make the shade's top and bottom borders look more expensive (and less synthetic), I covered them with a band of preppy-looking burgundy and gold striped ribbon.

START YOUR LAMPSHADE DECOR BY BORDERING THE ROUND TOP AND BOTTOM EDGES WITH A NARROW TRIM, PREFERABLY AN EIGHTH OF AN INCH WIDE. A ribbon, band, or cord that is more than half an inch wide will not work, as it will not lie flat.

If you like the look of a very wide band of trim, glue gun several narrow ribbons or cords one above the other. Ribbon trim can also be applied vertically; I recently rescued a pleated plastic shade by gluing twenty strips of navy blue ribbon in neat, regular vertical stripes onto it.

If you want to add cut-out fabric flowers, leaves, or geometric motifs to your paper or cloth shades, space them apart so that the light shows through in between the patterns. Densely layered embroidered bits will cut down the light dramatically. (Metal or raffia shades can be covered head to toe, because they are opaque; the light will not be affected.)

When you attach trim and patterns to tiny chandelier shades, remember that less is more: Keep it light and simple. Those four, six, or eight shades will all be lit up close together, so give all of them the same exact trim and pattern treatment. Finally, never glue anything to the interior of a lampshade—the heat from a lightbulb can soften and even melt your glue. It might also warp or burn the trim.

3

TIP THREE: Here's a quick trick I learned from Keith Langham, one of America's most colorful and charming decorators. To spruce up a black trim or border on a lampshade (or a piece of furniture or even a rug), simply draw over the faded, stained, or scratched parts with a black felt-tip pen. You can also use felt-tip pens (carefully!) to hide glue smears on ribbon or cord trim. The trick is to match the color of the ink as closely as possible to the color of the surface you're trying to improve.

TIP FOUR: I love this hexagonal lampshade because it looks so crisp and tailored. To make it look even more architectural, I decided to emphasize each of its six facets. I chose a Kelly green ribbon trim that I had purchased on eBay last year. I measured out twenty-four pieces of ribbon (four for each of the six panels) and pinned them into place before I started gluing. Because grosgrain ribbon unravels easily, I sealed the cut ends with Aleene's Stop Fraying.

3 | SOFAS & CHAIRS

Painting your walls a new color is the most dramatic decorative change you can make, but re-covering furniture comes in a close second. I can't think of any decor spruce-up that's as satisfying as covering a tired old warhorse of a chair or sofa with a fresh layer of material and trim. Even if I could afford endless rounds of "couture" reupholstery, I would still want to change or add new details myself.

It's probably more prudent to stick with the orphans you find at auctions, antiques fairs, and flea markets. Throughout fifteen years of editing decorating magazines, I have met lots of people who collect fine furniture. They're not just connoisseurs; they are guardians who respect, maintain, and preserve some of the most extraordinarily made objects in the world. It's demanding, hard work! And it's not for me.

This nineteenth-century French daybed traveled with me from Paris to New York; I have re-covered it at least four times over sixteen years. The current rehab is a combination of plain black cotton muslin used to cover the sides; a bright red wool and linen blend for the wide, deep cushion; and many yards of tan wool braid and red elastic trims that I found on eBay. The trims hide many sins, including glue marks and old nail heads that I couldn't remove. The pillows are decorated with cut-out flowers and squiggles from several antique Suzanis.

LIKE SO MANY OTHER PEOPLE WHO HAVE TO WATCH HOW THEY SPEND THEIR MONEY, I LIVE HAPPILY WITH FURNITURE THAT WON'T BE DEFILED BY THE HAZARDS OF MY DAY-TO-DAY LIFE. Exuberant friends who spill red wine; a constant stream of houseguests with muddy boots and wet bathing suits; my neighbors' shedding dogs; my niece's curtain-climbing cat; ceilings that leak; thirty-four steaming, sputtering radiators; and weekly dinner parties lit up by three dozen dripping candles don't exactly complement delicate furnishings. In fact, my life would be hell if I had to worry about soiling a Jean-Michel Frank settee or spilling chocolate sauce on an eighteenth-century armchair. If my lifestyle means that I have to re-cover my upholstered furniture every other year, so be it.

I started transforming furniture when I lived in Paris in the 1970s and '80s. My then-husband and I lived in a big, airy apartment with lots of rooms that needed lots of furniture. I scoured the Clignancourt and Port de Vanves flea markets almost every weekend, eventually amassing rooms full of tattered side chairs, saggy sofas, dinged consoles, scratched dining tables, nicked dressing tables, and wobbly china cabinets. I regarded all of them as potential treasures; they just needed a bit of strategic repair and pampering. Every one had redeeming qualities—something special about each piece's distinctive shape or whimsical color or graceful legs or impressive size that far outweighed the wear-and-tear factor. I learned how to sand down rough wood, apply a thin coat of veneer, stabilize creaky legs, and, best of all, cover up tattered fabric.

These two tall baroque beauties are my all-time favorite chairs. They looked so forlorn and ugly when I spotted them at a local auction preview that I almost didn't leave a bid. I had very mixed feelings when I got the pair for less than six hundred dollars. They were total wrecks, so I shipped them off to a professional upholsterer, who actually gasped when she received them.

Five months later, they were stabilized, firmly padded, and covered in solid white cotton muslin. All I had to do was add two rows of braided upholstery trim around the edges. But, not surprisingly, I decided to take them a step further, so I cut out several swirly, scalloped floral designs from an old Suzani textile.

The project took me several days because the edges of the embroideries were as jagged and irregular as hairpin curves: If there are a lot of twists and turns, you've got to maneuver slowly!

WHEN I MOVED TO NEW YORK CITY IN THE 1990's, MY "FURNITURE REHAB HABIT" WENT INTO HIGH GEAR AFTER MY GLUE GUNNING GRADUATED FROM A HOBBY TO A LIFELINE. I started cautiously enough: The solid gray satin seat cushions on my twelve ebonized black wood dining chairs were square and simple—and they desperately needed to be re-covered. I popped the seats out from their frames and spent hours carefully snipping and ripping off faded gray satin so that I could apply new, zany coral floral cotton. Once I had stripped them down to their metal-coil and cotton-batting bases, I realized that I could have simply left the gray satin in place and glue gunned the new fabric over, around, and under it.

A professional upholsterer would have a fit with the technique (or lack thereof) I began to develop, but the results looked neat and tailored. I taught myself how to tuck and fold fabric over corners, around curved edges and into tight spots. I learned how to tuck tiny pleats of fabric around flat straight-edged chair backs. I can even glue new fabric over and around large rolled sofa arms. Throughout the fifteen or so years I've been "re-covering," I've given seven stools, six hall chairs, five wing chairs, seven sofas, forty-one dining chairs, two settees, eleven armchairs, eight headboards, and a gazillion cushions and pillows a new look and a new life.

(left) It looks as if someone spilled a mug full of coffee over the seat of this fine English wooden chair. (Someone appeared to have smeared nail polish and lipstick over it, too!) When I found it in a New York City antique shop, I loved the clean graphic lines and the Oriental look of the back, but I thought the seat needed some graphic interest to balance the strong geometric back.

(above) I found a piece of pale celadon linen that was the right size—a yard square—and just the right background for this four-pronged embroidered design. I used a pair of manicure scissors and a mat knife to extract it from its red cotton background. I applied Aleene's Stop Fraying glue to the edges, waited for it to dry, and then pinned it into place on the seat. Hot gluing it down took longer than I expected: Each of the sixty petals had to be secured from tip to base.

When I found it at an auction in New Orleans, this dramatic neo-Gothic armchair was covered in a repellant, stubborn layer of dirty pink brocade, but I knew it would sell for a tidy sum because of its size and wonderful turned-wood details. I left a hefty bid, got it, and set to work.

STEP ONE: First, I deepened the wood color from grungy, muddy brown to flat black by applying two coats of Kiwi black shoe polish. After it dried, I covered the seat and back in heavy cotton duck, which complements the chair's girth and heft.

STEP TWO: When I considered my embroidery embellishment options, I was stymied. The design of the turned wood was so strong that almost any embroidered flower or vine or leaf I put near it faded away fast. And then I remembered the pillows I had recently found in a souk in Marrakech. One of them was the source of this circular, Arabic-looking embroidery on the seat back.

49

RE-COVERING IS NOT REUPHOLSTERING. When I find a piece of furniture with its stuffing falling out or its coils flattened and brittle, I call in the pros to rebuild. I always ask them to cover everything in plain white cotton muslin so that I can add on and cover over. The repaired pieces usually come back with the fabric held in place with tiny upholstery nails. I simply add a border or two of braided trim or elastic to cover the nails and then proceed to embellish the seat cushions and backs with whatever embroidered or appliquéd tidbit I fancy at the moment. Some types of upholstery are too complicated to re-cover—anything tufted, most pieces without frames or borders, cushions that cannot be removed, and most furniture with puffy, curvy shapes. The pieces shown in this chapter were, by and large, straightforward re-covering projects. Some of them are over fourteen years old, and they've held up beautifully.

A beloved, beat-up fabric sofa can be quickly spiffed up if you simply re-cover the seat cushion. You might try using a contrasting color to give it a modern, graphic appeal. Measure out the amount of fabric you need to cover the cushion on top, on the sides, and about six inches or so to wrap and stretch well under the bottom. Use a long, slanted nozzle to hot glue the new fabric into place by applying a steady stream, in two-inch increments, right above and below each line of piping on all four sides of the cushion. Get the glue as close to the piping as possible, but not on it. Flatten excess fabric into neat little tucks on each side of each corner, and secure them on the underside of the cushion. Add rows of contrasting elastic or braided trim to cover up the glue lines around all corded borders.

Glue-gun decorating ranges from quick, straight detailing with ribbons or cords to more complicated applications of intricately shaped embroidered forms. The sofa pictured here is one of the simplest glue-gun projects I've ever done. It took only twenty minutes to hot glue two concentric lines of upholstery braid up the front of the arms and up over the seams between the sides and the back.

FOR GLUE-GUN BEGINNERS, POP-OUT SEAT CUSHIONS ON OCCASIONAL, DESK, OR DINING CHAIRS ARE THE EASIEST CANDIDATES FOR RE-COVERING. Most upholstered seats are screwed in place underneath, so you must unscrew them and then prod gently (bang with your fist, not a hammer) until the seat separates from the frame. Measure out the amount of fabric you need to completely cover the seat, plus three or four inches to fold under the bottom edges to keep it secure. Cut the fabric in a form that follows the shape of the seat and, using the pointed nozzle on your glue gun, begin gluing at the middle of the back edge of the seat. Stretch the fabric taut but not too tight, over the front of the seat and then glue it in the middle of the front outer edge. Do the same for the sides. Once those four points have been attached, work out from the center of each side, leaving the four corners until last. Gather the excess fabric up and then tuck and pleat it on either side of each corner. Try to arrange matching pleats and tucks on all eight sides of the four corners for a seamless, symmetrical look. Finish off by securing the fabric to the underside of the seat with a generous amount of hot glue. You will need to attach it very firmly, as seats have to take a lot of tension; don't scrimp on the glue sticks.

(above) This neo-Gothic child's chair looked so unloved when I found it in a friend's garage, covered with leaves and spiderwebs. The original needlepoint upholstery was rotting and torn. The stuffing and webbing were spilling out; the black ebonized wood was splotched with white paint; and one of the brass caster feet was missing: This was total rehab.

(opposite) Here's the chair a month later. I replaced the caster, padded the seat top, glued the needlepoint back into place, and then covered all the upholstered areas with a new fabric.

The four photos (opposite) show how I applied a pleated silk panel to cover the bare webbing on the back of the chair.

STEP 1: Before I pinned the fabric to the webbing, I covered the white paint splotches with three applications of Kiwi's black shoe polish. I used the attached sponge applicator, but I also used a small paintbrush to touch up small, hard-to-reach spots. Remember to always apply paint or Kiwi's to wood before you re-cover.

STEP TWO: The area to be covered was about eight inches wide, and I knew I would need three times as much fabric to make generous pleats. I cut a width of twenty-four inches from a yard of beige crepe de chine. Then I cut the fabric to roughly the same length as the webbed area.

STEP THREE: Starting from the center, moving first to the left then to the right, I tucked the fabric into pleats straight from the top to the bottom and secured the ends of each pleat with a pin. In the middle, I made a wide pleat to add focus. Removing one pin at a time, I glue gunned first the top part of the pleat and then the bottom, pulling the fabric into place if it shifted.

STEP FOUR: I neatened up the edges and hid the areas that were glue gunned. The most forgiving trim to use is elastic; in this case, two feet of a half-inch ribbed matte black band did the trick. I applied the hot glue to both the elastic and the fabric for extra staying power.

SIDE CHAIRS AND DINING CHAIRS ARE PARTICULARLY GOOD CANDIDATES FOR EMBROIDERED EMBELLISH-MENTS. Leave club chairs alone, and zaftig wing chairs might be better off at an upholsterer's as well. If your seat cushion is large, dress it up with a similarly big embroidered pattern, placed in the middle of the seat, or with four smaller bits arranged at the corners. As chair seats will get more use than chair backs or sides, make sure you apply enough hot glue to keep everything in place.

You might want to have the body of your tailored sofa re-covered by a pro, but you can still add a bit of trim yourself. When I purchased my barrel-like Ralph Lauren sofa, it was covered in plain white muslin (see page 30). It looked great, and I wanted to leave it plain and calm, but also wanted to add a bit of something that would tie it in to the other furniture in the room. I decided that all it needed to fit in was a bit of red-and-black braided cord running up the front of the arms. In twenty minutes, my sofa was personalized and minimally but uniquely embellished. The best fabrics for re-covering most chairs are not too thick. Plush chenille and slubby wool tweeds are hard to work around corners and under edges. Go for cotton muslin, raw silk, and supple wools with a bit of "give" to them. I do not like heavy brocades or damasks; I think they make everything look old and old-fashioned. Light and lightweight is the way to go. If you will be re-covering very straight-lined square seats and backs, cotton duck, awning fabric, and mattress ticking can look crisp and chic.

(left) This chic, plushly padded dressing room chair was in pretty good shape when I found it. I love the caramel-colored paisley patterns and the rustic look of the off-white wool fabric.

(above) It didn't take long to cover over the torn seam in the crease between the seat and back, and the stuffing that was falling out of the bottom was quickly put back into place with a tiny amount of hot glue. To cover over the rough seams and holes, I used a thick wool braided trim and glued it from side to side and then around the seat back as well. Just for fun, I added a bow.

(left) This is one of a pair of not very comfortable, but fun to look at Eastlake chairs that I had shipped to New York from an antiques fair in San Clemente, California. They were beautifully upholstered in white muslin, and they stayed pretty clean for about a year. One party too many later, the red wine and Diet Coke stains took their toll. Rehab time. Although this looks like a simple glue-gun decorating project, it was difficult.

(above) The arms were particularly tough to make look neat and professional. I chose a fabric that I thought would be easy to work with: loosely woven, fairly thick, flecked beige linen. It had a nice give and stretch to it, so I could pull and nudge it into place as I glue gunned. I added two rows of elastic trim and decorated the seat cushion and back with large circular designs cut out from a Suzani cloth.

(left) This sculptural little chair manufactured by Baker Furniture is one of a group of twelve. It was designed to sit in a hall, not at a dining table, so it was cushionless. I loved the tulip shape of the back and the graceful curves of the legs, but I knew it would be uncomfortable to sit on for more than twenty minutes.

(above) Solution? Add a layer of softness. I found twelve inexpensive foam-filled cushions online for seven dollars apiece. Their French provincial print didn't thrill me, so I re-covered them with cut-up pieces from an old French bedspread. I cut the pieces to the shape of the top of the cushions, glued them down around all edges, cut off the excess fabric, and then covered up the raw cut edges with a black braided cord. To keep the loose cushions in place, I applied four dabs of hot glue to the four corners of each wooden seat and then pressed the cushions into place. They haven't budged in two years!

This shapely dressing table went through several fabric maneuvers before it landed a starring role in my country house bedroom. I covered the plain wood top with rich hot pink cotton and then attached a skirt made from four yards of tucked twenty-seven-inch widths of white cotton muslin to the sides of the tabletop. As there were lots of visible glue marks (the cotton muslin was very thin, and the glue showed through), I used several rows of trim to cover them up. At the top and bottom of the skirt, which just grazes the floor, I added a four-inch border of tasseled printed cotton rescued from a faded antique Indian tablecloth.

Glue gunning fabric produces permanent results that are stronger, and often more durable, than bonds you can rig up using a sewing machine, a staple gun, or upholstery nails. You can hot glue almost any fabric to almost any hard or pliable element (including wood, Corian, wicker, metal, and padded upholstery), but certain fabrics are not suitable for hot gluing to anything. Loosely woven or knitted materials have too many holes that allow the glue to seep through. Chunky tweeds and coat-weight wool melton—as well as delicate, sheer silks and organzas—are not good candidates, either, because thick fabric feels and looks bulky when glued and sheer fabrics wrinkle and show glue marks. Synthetic fabrics are problematic; they warp, or even melt, on contact with hot glue. The best glue-gun-friendly yardages are tightly woven.

BEYOND MAKING CURTAINS OR RE-COVERING SOFAS AND CHAIRS, YOU CAN HOT GLUE FABRICS TO DRESSING-TABLE TOPS TO MAKE SKIRTS, TO BEDROOM WALLS TO MAKE INSTANT HEADBOARDS, AND TO THE BOTTOM STRETCHERS OF SOFAS TO MAKE PUFFY OR TAILORED SKIRT PANELS. If you want to launder your table skirts or instant headboards, you must use Aleene's Fabric Glue Sticks, which are harder to find. (Try your local craft stores and check their web sites as well.) Carefully peel off the panel or skirt from its base. Launder in cold water, dry, and re-glue. Do not iron out the creases—use a hand-held steamer.

When gluing fabrics to tables or across the bottoms of sofas, you will be tucking your yardage, inch by inch, doubling back and forth, to ensure that your skirts have a full, graceful look. If, for example, the dressing table you want to skirt is six feet in circumference, plan on using an eighteen-foot-long piece of fabric. As for how much fabric you need from the floor to the top of the surface you are working on, measure the space between the floor and top and add an extra inch or two. Always start attaching table skirts from the center of the backside, so that the slit between the beginning and the end segment is out of sight. Start by hot gluing one inch of fabric directly onto the side of the tabletop; let it cool and then double back, gluing an inch of fabric onto the fabric that you have already adhered. Advance one inch at a time, repeating the process, over and over, until the dressing table is completely surrounded with evenly tucked fabric. The slit that will occur in the back can either be glue gunned closed or left open, with both sides trimmed in cord, ribbon, or braid.

After the skirt is attached, cut off the excess fabric at the bottom, around the circumference, so that it barely brushes the floor. Add one or two rows of ribbon or trim to hide the cut edge. Do the same for the edge that is glue gunned to the top of the table.

Table skirts can give any old warhorse of a table a new life. This small table had spent most of its decorative existence painted Swedish gray. It was languishing in a guest room, and I needed a small round table in my entryway, so a transformation was in order.

STEP ONE: After spraying with two coats of black enamel paint, I measured the circumference of the table—seventy-five inches—and then tripled it to determine how much fabric I would need. Approximately four yards of hot pink cotton eyelet did the trick. I cut the length of the skirt twenty-seven inches, so that it brushed the floor.

STEP TWO: (opposite) I started gluing by attaching the upper edge of the cotton to the side of the tabletop.

STEP THREE: (above) "Glue and tuck" skirting works on literally any table shape. Tables with corners need skirts with extra—and extra wide—tucks on both sides of each corner. All loose ends and threads can be cut off or covered up later with trim.

TIP: Make sure your trims have heft and texture: A delicate border of satin ribbon will show glue marks and ridges. If you glue a heavy cord or braid around the hem, it will make the skirt fall nicely and stay in place.

(left and above) I found this inexpensive dressing room settee at an antique shop in Greenwich Village. It was covered in a pale blue moiré silk, but I wanted something with more oomph to jazz up an empty corner in my bedroom. I bought eight yards of periwinkle blue cotton twill and twelve yards of military-red elastic trim. After re-covering the settee (an arduous ordeal because of all the curves and the sturdy twill), I decided that it needed a skirt to make it more romantic.

The fourteen-inch-wide skirt was attached to the bottom of the seat and falls to the floor. I hot glued it straight across the front and added two very deep tucks (about two inches wide) at either side of each corner. To cover up the bottom edge, I attached a band of tasseled printed cotton culled from an antique Indian tablecloth. This is not a perfect glue-gun job, but I think it's pert and pretty, despite the puckers.

TO ADD SKIRTS TO THE BOTTOM OF SOFAS, first measure the distance between the floor and the bottom of the sofa front stretcher (the wooden segment that runs horizontally across the front). Whether it is five inches or fifteen inches, attach the skirt only after the rest of the sofa has been re-covered. For a frilly, girly look, tuck the fabric into tiny folds a third of an inch wide so that when it is glued into place, it actually looks gathered. If you want a more tailored look, apply the fabric straight (but not too tightly) across the front and tuck it, in two one-inch increments, on either side of all corners. This will allow your tailored skirt to "move" and "breathe" without too much froufrou. Finish both the top and bottom edges of the sofa skirt with trim.

Favorite bedside or occasional tables can take a beating, and if the tops are woven of straw or caned, repair workcan be mighty expensive. Consider an SOS glue-gun treatment. I recently rescued a pair of woven raffia double-decker bedside tables that I had used in eight different bedrooms over the course of more than fifteen years. I knew they would be almost impossible to replace because they were fifty years old and the perfect height and width for accommodating all my reading and writing materials; two very large lamps; and big trays loaded with water, CD players, and treats. Even though they were severely ripped, stained, and scratched, they were salvageable. I would simply have to re-cover them. I headed for the outdoor furniture upholstery section of my local fabric store and selected a stiff striped cotton ticking designed for use on patio furniture and awnings. It was waterproof and stain-resistant, so I figured it would be perfect for tables that get used every day and night. It was also just the right hefty material for gluing over a textured surface like raffia—the pattern of the straw would not show through.

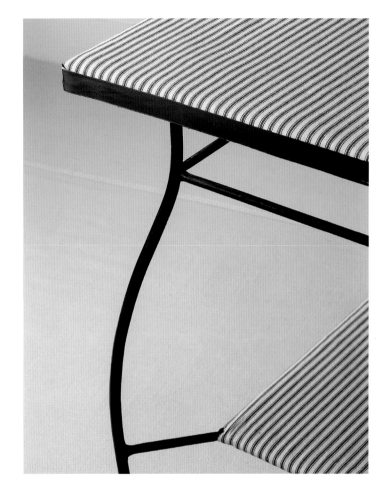

(left) This "before" shot of a favorite bedside table is pretty grim. The white woven straw was a little saggy, and numerous tea and makeup stains made it look even worse.

(above) It's amazing what a layer of ticking can do! I stretched the waterproof fabric over and under the top, as well as over the small portion on the bottom. I used a black grosgrain ribbon trim to finish it off.

61

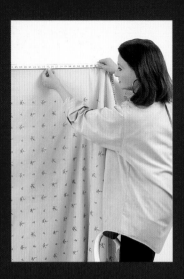

STEP ONE: *(above)* From a bolt of very wide linen, I measured out 123 inches (three times forty-one) and attached the middle forty-one inches to the wall behind the bed. Because I was after a dramatic, vertical look, I decided to make the headboard tall. I attached it five feet above the bed.

STEP TWO: After the middle section was hot glued to the wall, the two side sections hung down in natural folds.

STEP THREE: I hot glued twenty-eight pinecones, in varying sizes, across the top of the "instant" headboard to create a crown effect.

STEP FOUR: I attached a long braided silk cord that I knotted every inch or so to give it a thicker, coarser look. I attached four pinecone "tassels" to the ends to match the pinecone crown.

I CAME UP WITH THE IDEA OF AN "INSTANT HEADBOARD" HOURS BEFORE ONE HOUSEGUEST TOO MANY SHOWED UP FOR A LONG WEEKEND. My leaky old farmhouse did indeed boast ten bedrooms, but one of them was not exactly a looker, and it certainly wasn't comfortable. Rugless, curtainless, closetless, and way up on the third floor, in the attic, the only good things it had going for it were a firm twin bed and a great view. To give the room some charm and focus, I devised an instant headboard made of several yards of printed linen, a layer of synthetic fiberfill, thirty pinecones, and five yards of red braided trim. The bed was forty inches wide, so I figured I would need three times as much fabric.

I got 123 inches' worth of fabric and divided and marked it into three sections of forty-one inches each. I wanted the headboard to rise about five feet over the top of the bed, so I measured out five feet of fabric, plus another ten inches that would not reach the floor but would fall low enough to be hidden by the back of the bed. I tacked the middle forty-one-inch section to the wall directly above the bed. The two lengths of forty-one inches on either side fell into nice, full folds. Then I attached the bottom edges of the fabric to the wall near the floor and shoved a layer of soft, inch-thick cotton batting (which I had cut into a piece measuring thirty-six by fifty-five inches) in between the fabric and the wall.

When the fabric directly behind and above the bed looked smooth and slightly taut, I glue gunned the top edge of the middle forty-one-inch section directly to the wall with a generous amount of hot glue (about twice as thick as I normally would use). I attached a row of twenty-eight pinecones on top of the glue-gunned fabric edge, arranged with the largest one in the middle and smallest ones at the sides. (Use the pointed, slanted nozzle to apply hot glue from the top to the bottom of one side of each pinecone, on as many "petals" as possible.) After gluing the pinecones in a neat, symmetrical row, I covered the top edge of the fabric, right below the bottom of the pinecones, with a line of fat red cord. I left a length of about a foot and half of cord dangling from each side and attached two pinecones to each end—for an extra passementerie touch.

All in all, glue-gunned fabric maneuvers can be dramatic and fun. But they don't always take the place of sewing. I recently hot glued embroidery, ribbons, and appliqués to a cotton bedspread. After several washings and lots of day-to-day pulling and folding, it started to look a little tatty, and the ribbon trim lost its luster and grip. Bedspreads—or anything else that you need to launder frequently—are not ideal for glue-gun adventures.

This "instant headboard" made a tiny little attic bedroom look special and fun. I used about three and a half yards of seventy-inch vintage linen, twenty-nine pinecones, two yards of cotton batting, and four and a half yards of red braided cord. Assembly time required: one hour.

The little twin bed I wanted to glamorize was forty inches wide, so I made my instant headboard slightly bigger, forty-one inches wide.

TIP: I wouldn't try this with a full, queen- or king-sized bed. Even if you found a piece of fabric large enough, it would be difficult to hang it in a crease- and fold-free way. And, applying batting underneath would be a frustrating process indeed.

One-of-a-kind curtains and roller shades can make a mighty impressive decorative statement. They can give a room that "done by a professional interior designer" look. There are oodles of ready-made curtains available on Web sites and in home decorating and renovation stores, but the uniquely detailed curtains and shades you can glue gun yourself are far more satisfying and effective. And it's much cheaper than having a seamstress, tailor, or decorator make them for you!

Curtain panels are a great way to show off your glue-gunning acumen. Measure your fabric from the top edge of the rod to the floor and then add two inches more for hemming and attaching hooks or rings. Lay the fabric flat on a long table and glue ribbon, cord, or braid to the long vertical edges. Then apply embroidered motifs, in a regular, repetitive line, down one or both sides of the panel. After attaching the panel to the rod, you can add a bowed, tassled cord to finish it off.

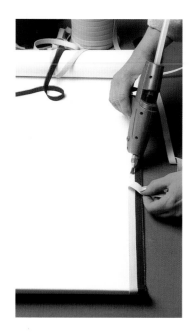

Transforming a basic plastic roller shade requires about ten yards of elastic trim (at a cost of about ten dollars) and forty-five minutes. I found this standard-issue shade at my local hardware store for about six dollars.

STEP ONE: Starting with the outside edge first, I glued a strip of half-inch dark blue elastic to the left, right, and bottom.

STEP TWO: (above) After the dark blue elastic was in place, I added another stripe of lighter blue trim to all three sides.

STEP THREE: (opposite) I liked the regimented stripes so much that I added a third one.

THE EASIEST, MOST BASIC WINDOW COVER YOU CAN DOLL UP IS A ROLLER SHADE. You can buy them either in canvas or plastic, cut to fit, at supermarkets to department stores. The plastic versions are the cheapest and the ugliest—and hence can benefit the most from glue-gun embellishing. In general, window shades look best when they're not overloaded with froufrou—a single or double border of ribbon or flat braid trim around all edges will transform them from banal necessities to snappy, chic decorative accessories. It will take about twenty minutes to attach a band of grosgrain ribbon half an inch or wider to the shade's left, right, and bottom edges (the bottom is usually wrapped around a wooden or plastic rod to weigh it down). This is one of the infrequent times that you should use the low, or "Regular," switch on your glue gun. When you work on plastic, sizzling hot glue can warp or burn it. Use the wide wedge nozzle to glue ribbon trim in straight lines on all three sides. If the trim is too thick, the shade will not roll up properly, so never use anything heftier than grosgrain to outline shades.

When you make curtain panels, decide whether you will need to launder them or not. How often will they be opened and closed? Will dogs, cats, and children come into contact with them? Are they going to hang in a busy kitchen or a seldom-used guestroom? Are they flanking a window or door that opens to the outside? If you answered yes to any of the above, standard glue sticks are not for you; they do not produce a bond that is washable or dry cleanable. You need Aleene's Fabric Glue Sticks. When you consider materials for your glue-gunned curtains, keep in mind that sheer synthetics are not suitable (the glue marks show through) and heavy brocade and velvets are too weighty and serious for glue-gun decorating. I have found that medium-weight cotton muslin (a couple of dollars a yard in any fabric shop) is the ideal base cloth for glue gunning. I buy it by the bolt because I tend to replace all my curtains every other year. And remember that each curtain panel you glue gun will have to be lined with another panel length of fabric because glue marks show through to the back.

COTTON MUSLIN COMES IN A PANOPLY OF COLORS. Choose one that echoes the color of your walls or vividly contrasts with it. When in doubt, take the white route: If your room has bright white moldings, ceiling, doors, and window surrounds, go with pure white cotton. If your room has no white woodwork, go with off-white muslin. Beigy white looks more antique and lived-in; snowy white looks crisper, newer, and more contemporary.

Muslin can be purchased in bolts of up to fifty yards and in a standard width of about thirty-five inches. You will need to decide how full a curtain effect you want. Picture or bowed windows will need four or more panels. Standard thirty-four-inch-wide windows require two panels each. If you want to create a fluffier, layered, or dense window treatment for your picture window, you will need six panels or more.

All edges of the panels—top, bottom, and sides—have to be trimmed with ribbon, braid, or cord. That's a lot of trim! For example, a pair of curtains that are each thirty-five inches wide and eighty-six inches long will eat up about 496 inches, or approximately forty-two feet, of trim—a potential financial disaster. I recommend logging on to eBay to buy ribbon, cord, or elastic trim in bulk from sellers who specialize in factory closeouts. I have found numerous reels of from ten to one hundred yards of trim for prices ranging from five to thirty-five dollars per reel. I regularly search the "sewing" and "arts and crafts" sections of eBay to buy large lots of trims when they come up for auction. Even if I don't need them for a current project, I add them to a "trim reserve" that will come in handy later. Remember that sheer ribbon will not work on your glue-gun projects. (It's too delicate, and the glue marks will show through.) Go for grosgrain or moiré ribbon; wool, silk, or cotton braided upholstery trim; or strips of ribbed elastic. Also remember that for curtains you're less likely to need narrow ribbons, yarn, and silk cords—they're too subtle. Buy most of your curtain trims in widths of half an inch or more.

(bottom left) What could be more basic than a bolt of cotton muslin? It comes in an array of colors from pale pink to deep blue, and it costs about two dollars a yard. If your windows are about thirty-four inches wide by seventy-six inches long, your curtain material will cost around eleven dollars a pair. Get the medium- or heavyweight muslin; the lightweight stuff is too flimsy.

STEP ONE: *(bottom right)* After spreading your curtain material flat on a long dining table or desk, apply ribbon trim to the outside edge of all sides. Use Aleene's flat wedge-shaped glue gun nozzle with multiple small holes; it is designed to distribute a thin trail of ribbon-friendly hot glue about half an inch wide. Make sure that you glue your ribbon, braid, or elastic exactly to the outer edge of the fabric so that it is completely covered. After gluing down all four sides, you may want to add a second row of trim. Hot glue it either right up against the first, or leave a quarter of an inch of fabric between the two for an airier look. Corners require special attention; cut all trim and ribbon edges with a pair of scissors.

STEP TWO: *(opposite)* After gluing down two rows of ribbon trim on the muslin curtain panel, I laid several dozen cut-out embroidered motifs in place and anchored the smaller bits with pins. I started glue gunning in a corner on a large piece. After affixing the center of the circular design, I carefully lifted up the sides and glued from the inside out, adhering the tiny, outer edges last.

MY ALL-TIME FAVORITE EMBROIDERED MATERIALS ARE SUZANIS—THE BRIGHT FLORAL AND GEOMETRIC-PATTERNED EMBROIDERED COTTON CLOTHS HAND-SEWN BY WOMEN IN UZBEKISTAN FOR CENTURIES. About sixty of them, sold by textile dealers throughout the world, are featured on eBay at any given hour of the day. The appeal of Suzanis is the size and color of the embroideries. Some of the circular motifs are a foot in diameter and colored in bright peacock blue, crimson, spring green, and lemon yellow. A typical Suzani incorporates flowers, leaves, and vines, as well as graphic circles, zigzags, and squiggles that are bold and cheerful. When I buy a Suzani cloth on eBay, I double-check the size (it must be at least five feet long to incorporate ample embroideries), and I always note the seller's description of the condition of the piece. If it is a well-preserved antique Suzani, it's a shame to cut it up. Look for descriptions including "worn," "faded," "some rips," or "frayed portions" to help you find what you're after. Prices vary widely depending on age, condition, and the level of sophisticated stitching. Garishly colored machine-made Suzanis (dating from the 1970s to the present) are cheaper than handmade ones. Suzanis embroidered in pale, subtle colors are more expensive than those with bright colors. The smaller and more densely packed the stitches, the higher the price tag. I try not to spend more than two hundred dollars for a large (up to ten-foot-long) Suzani with enough embroidery to cut out and apply to four pairs of curtain panels. Any way you divide it, that's quite a deal! For instructions on how to select, cut out, secure, and glue down embroidered and appliquéd motifs, see chapter 2.

STEP ONE: You need steady hands and lots of patience to cut out embroidered bits as complicated as this one. And if you want to extract artfully stitched patterns from an old, fragile Suzani cloth, you need a few trusty allies as well—bright, even light; a pair of reading glasses; and, perhaps most important of all, a very good pair of manicure scissors to navigate all of the curves and swerves. Never cut too close to the embroidery. If you cut into the stitches, they will unravel. Leave about a sixteenth of an inch of the cotton base cloth around each embroidered motif to keep it intact.

STEP TWO: When cutting out embroidered flowers, leaves, or geometric motifs from cotton cloths, you might find it helpful to use a razor-sharp mat knife with a pointed edge. Make sure the blade is clean and new, so that it won't rip the fabric.

STEP THREE: After you have cut out your embroidered flower or leaf or squiggle from its mother cloth, trim the cloth close to the embroidery and apply small dabs of Aleene's Stop Fraying glue to all edges with the aid of a small natural-bristle paintbrush. When you apply the liquid glue, it is bluish-white in color. When it dries, about fifteen or so minutes later, it is almost clear, with a slight sheen.

ALWAYS TRIM YOUR CURTAINS IN A TONE THAT CONTRASTS WITH THE COLOR OF THE FABRIC AND THAT WILL ALSO COMPLEMENT OR ECHO A COLOR THAT FIGURES PROMINENTLY IN THE ROOM. For instance, if you are trimming a pair of red cotton curtains in a room with white walls and dark mahogany furniture, you might want to trim the panels in white and black. This both outlines the curtains and reflects the other colors in the room. If your white curtain panels are destined to hang in a pale blue room, try trimming them in pale lavender or sea foam blue-green for a subtle contrast.

If you want to take your curtains a step beyond discreet trim, consider adding bits of cut-out embroidery or appliqués near the bottom and sides. You will most likely need plenty of artillery to embellish a pair of thirty-four-inch-wide curtain panels, so start by searching for fairly identical embroidered bits in multiples. Two or three embroidered pansies, no matter how colorful and pretty, will not look like much glued to the bottoms of a pair of curtain panels. You need at least twenty-four similar embroidered bits to make a good-looking pair of glue-gunned curtains. My favorite source of embroidery is—again—eBay. And aside from the occasional lucky find at an antique shop or auction, the embroidery-laden fabrics I regularly find online are priced so well that I can buy them in multiples and stockpile them. I click into the "antique" section, then into "textiles" and then type in the words "embroidery" or "embroidered," and I almost always find a hundred or more fabrics bearing hand-stitched flowers, animals, leaves, fruits, and geometric patterns. Some of the textiles are old tablecloths, wall hangings, bed covers, and draperies; some are smaller items such as tea towels, pillowcases, and handkerchiefs. I skip all smaller items because I need more than a couple of pieces of embroidery from the same source to decorate a pair of curtains; I want my motifs to match or at least be of similar patterns and colors. Only a large tablecloth, wall hanging, or bedspread provides the necessary artillery.

(opposite) Here's a group of nine Suzani embroideries at various stages of being cut out. Hand stitched in yellow, green, black, and white, all were taken from the same red cotton Suzani cloth, and all of them ended up on the same pair of curtains. When selecting which embroideries you will use for a pair of curtains, make sure that the designs and colors are similar, if not matching. You do not want to use two or three or more disparate types of embroidery on one pair of curtains; they will look messy and unplanned.

Ever since I was old enough to climb a ladder, I've thought of plain painted walls as big beautiful "canvases" ready to be drawn on, painted on, or, most fun of all, glue gunned on. Hand-done murals can give even the most ordinary, pokey little room a real "wow" factor. Making your own murals and nature pictures is a deeply satisfying glue-gun adventure, but it's also arduous. If you want your patterns—featuring shells, leaves, pinecones, acorns, wheat shafts, thistles, seeds, pods, or anything else that nature leaves on the ground—to be ravishing, they must be well-planned and carefully executed.

Fifteen years ago, I encrusted a giant, ugly New York City fireplace with several hundred white seashells. I soon realized that the shell theme could be further developed. So I turned a windowed nook into a grotto and embellished the dining room ceiling with shell borders and medallions.

To add drama and depth to my New York City living room ceiling, I glue gunned several thousand shells (in varying sizes and shapes) around the periphery. In their natural colors, the shells added architecture, texture, and warmth to the room. For a touch of whimsy, and to play around with scale, I placed large sea urchins here and there. Their girth contrasted dramatically with the size of the smaller shells.

75

GLUE GUNNING SHELLS—PARTICULARLY THOSE OVER FOUR INCHES IN DIAMETER—IS A PRETTY IFFY AFFAIR. Big, heavy specimens, including conch, scallop, and abalone shells, need a considerable amount of hot glue to make them stick. Hot glue bonds are not weatherproof—something to remember if you live in a city where the climate changes dramatically from freezing to broiling. I've learned that it's safer to use smaller shells when decorating a wall or ceiling. Never work with species more than five inches long.

Before you start applying shells directly to your walls, make sure the paint is fresh and even and that the plaster is in good condition: a hot-glued shell will eventually fall off a wall covered in peeling paint or dry flaky plaster. Shells adhered to Sheetrock have better staying power. When you encrust a large wooden mirror or picture frame with shells, make sure that you sandpaper the surface, whether it is painted or not. Sanding removes the paint and veneer, revealing the porous grain underneath and ensuring a stronger glue bond.

Visually exciting shelled walls, ceilings, and frames display a good variety and quantity of shells. Combining at least five different types and sizes will give your work texture and density. For murals, sketch out a general design directly on the wall with a pencil. Plan where you want to use larger shells and where you will need smaller "filler" shells to add contrast and detail. Gather up more shells than you think you will need and group them into piles according to type and size. Using a pointed, slanted nozzle, glue gun the shells from top to bottom, making sure to cover all contact points with hot glue.

FOR FRAME PROJECTS, I MEASURE THE DIMENSIONS OF THE FRAME—SAY, SIX INCHES WIDE BY SIXTY INCHES LONG BY THIRTY INCHES ACROSS—AND THEN DO SOME ROUGH MATH. I multiply five times sixty to equal 300, and five times thirty to equal 150. I add the two together for a total of 450 shells—at least! And it's harder to determine a total shell count for large pieces like murals.

There are no design rules, but there are a few dos and don'ts that will help your shelling look sophisticated: Always start glue gunning shell patterns (as well as patterns incorporating pinecones, acorns, seeds, wheat shafts, pods, or thistles) in the center of the wall and then work out to both sides, switching often from the left to the right side to make sure that you achieve a symmetrical look. When you start gluing in the center of the wall, you're "grounded," and you stand a better chance of completing a balanced, logical design. Leaving space around each shell will give your mural a fresh, contemporary look; piling them up or overlapping them will look helter-skelter and amateurish.

Walls are perfect surfaces for creating nature murals, so I transformed a pale pink guest bedroom into a rustic fairytale "forest princess" room using several thousand pinecones, acorns, wheat shafts, thistles, and dried seeds and pods. It's taken six years of on-and-off glue gunning (and it's still not finished!); it's my number-one favorite project. Beware! This kind of glue-gun decorating is mighty effective, but it's also a magnet for dust and lint.

(opposite) Waking up in this soft pink, white, and pineconed bedroom is like waking up in a birthday cake—festive, fun, pretty, and sweet. I started my pinecone motif after I had glue gunned the white linen curtains to the window frames. (I was too lazy to hang them from rods.) The next step was to add big puffy pinecone swags at the corners. By the time I decided to decorate the walls with pinecones, I had come up with the idea of using both very tiny pinecones and little tied up bunches of weeds and seedpods. Anything growing in my garden and forest was fair game for this room.

(bottom left) Before I started gluing, I drew a general design, incorporating delicate swirls and dense, oval medallions, directly on the wall with a pencil. I started each design in the center of the wall and then worked out from there. The most prevalent elements are 1,050 mini pinecones, gathered from the ground under a

neighbor's huge weeping sergeant hemlock. Also front and center are about 850 acorns collected from another neighbor's lawn and driveway.

(botttom right) I couldn't resist finishing off a pair of country house curtains with pinecone "finials." As every wall (and even the ceiling) of this guestroom was covered with swirling pinecone patterns, I thought it was only fitting that the curtains get the pinecone treatment as well. I gathered up about fifteen pinecones three to four inches in length, then knotted each one with a twelve-inch-long piece of nylon fishing line around the top. I then pulled the lines until some of the cones were higher and some lower, forming a sort of irregular oval shape. When all the cones were in place, I knotted the lines together, hooked them over the white curtain rod holder, and glue gunned a chocolate brown grosgrain bow to the top.

TIP: All items or elements glue gunned to a wall must be clean and dried. If you apply green or moist branches, flowers, or seeds to a dry surface, they will either not adhere, or they will shrink, peel, and shred several weeks later.

ALTHOUGH NATURAL COLORED SHELLS CAN BE COMBINED IN BEAUTIFUL, SUBTLY CONTRASTING PATTERNS, PAINTING THE SHELLS ALL ONE COLOR—WHITE, OFF-WHITE, BLACK, OR TAN—TAKES THEM ONE STEP AWAY FROM THAT HONKY-TONK GIFT-SHOP LOOK THAT YOU WANT TO AVOID. It also emphasizes the beautiful lines and shapes of most seashells, large or small. To paint them, set up a large painter's tarp or length of kraft paper outdoors or in a well-ventilated room. Arrange the shells on the tarp so they do not touch each other. Using matte acrylic spray paint, coat them thoroughly. When the shells are dry, turn them over and repeat the process on the undersides.

If attaching shells directly to bare walls is too much of a decorative stretch for you, there's an easier, more portable way of decking out your walls with glue-gunned nature. Invest in a battery of picture frames, both with and without glass.

For shell pictures, choose sturdy wooden models with frames at least two inches wide. I recently found several baroque oval frames from the 1940s at an antique shop in Hudson, New York. Covered in dingy gray paint, scuffed up, and glassless, they were the perfect candidates for shell art. First I cleaned and sprayed the frames with matte black paint. Then I measured the insides and cut out one-eighth-inch-thick cardboard ovals to fit over the openings in the back. I sprayed one side of each cardboard oval with white matte paint and placed that side to the front. The brads on the backsides of the frames held the cardboard in place. After making sure that the cardboard-to-wood bond was tight and strong, I started gluing white-painted shells of six different sizes and styles (three-inch sand dollars, as well as tiny spirals and snails) in vaguely symmetrical patterns so that they covered the cardboard. Each frame held a different shell configuration and pattern, but they all worked together.

(bottom left) After your glassless frame has been backed with a piece of sturdy corrugated cardboard, painted white and glued onto the back of the frame, hot glue your shells into place in a symmetric pattern. Start in the center and work outward, covering the cardboard with shells from end to end. When gluing down a large scallop shell, be sure to apply hot glue to the entire perimeter and press it down firmly.

(bottom right) Two things make this shell picture come to life: the all-white shells of different sizes and shapes and the contrast of the black frame. I found seven of these frames at an antique shop in Hudson, New York. Nobody wanted them because they were backless and glassless, but they were just what I needed. At three dollars apiece, they were even more attractive.

(opposite) My New York City dining room featured a huge square fireplace. I painted it flat black and glue gunned about nine hundred white-painted shells to the surface.

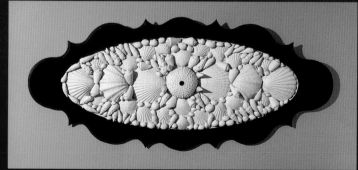

WORKING WITH DRIED, PRESSED LEAVES IS BOTH
EASIER AND MORE DIFFICULT THAN WORKING WITH
SHELLS. Dried leaves will never fall off the surface they are
glued to, but coaxing them into place with the right amount
of glue is a bear. So is gathering them up. You must collect
them in the autumn, when leaves start turning and falling.
You can't gather leaves in winter, and the green leaves
of spring and summer are too moist to dry and flatten
properly. Another leaf conundrum is that a dry leaf is light,
fragile, and brittle. It's tough to handle and even harder to
glue into place.

As is the case with shells, you will need several different varieties of leaves to construct an interesting picture.
Depending on where you live, go into action in October or
November to amass several hundred large specimens
(*Macleaya cordata* and catalpa), several hundred tiny ones
(Japanese maple, honeysuckle, sumac), and a thousand of
the middle-sized ones that you will use more than any other
size (oak, maple, elm, chestnut, birch). I don't have a professional flower press—I would need dozens. Instead I use
twenty or so old dog-eared coffee table books that I don't
care about. (Pressing leaves soils pages.) Between every ten
or so pages, I insert as many leaves as will fit if placed flat
so that they do not overlap. After filling up and closing the
books, I place them, stacked in groups of three or four,
under the legs of heavy tables, sofas, trunks, or storage
boxes. The leaves need about ten days to flatten and dry
out. Sometimes even ten days won't do the trick, so I remove
them from the book pages and iron them flat between two
dry paper towels, with the iron on medium heat.

(left and above) These two photos
show two standard poster frames
after they are filled and sealed up
with leaf designs. Notice that both
examples leave lots of air around
each leaf and bordering all sides.
The more space you leave between
your leaves, the fresher and more
modern your leaf pictures will look.

(opposite) These two oval ready-
made canvases were just the right
size for two paisley-shaped leaf
collages. What makes these two
designs a graphic success is the
amount of white space around the
edges. As I prefer to leave them
unshellacked, they won't last more
than a couple of months before
the leaves start cracking and disin-
tegrating. If you want your leaf
pictures to have staying power,
frame them under glass or acrylic.

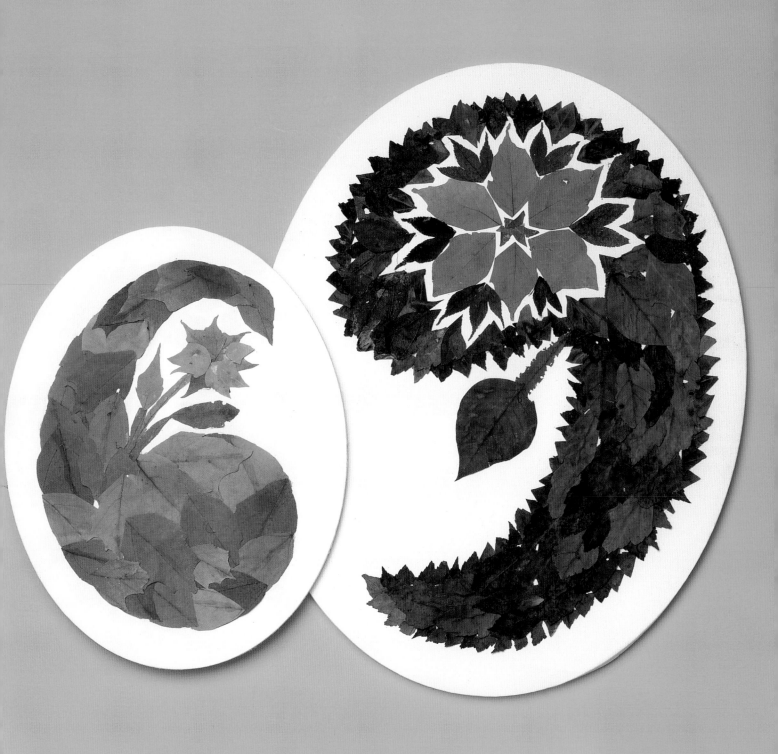

Before I hung these fifteen leaf pictures, my coral country dining room felt too vast and looked too dark. By hanging framed and unframed canvases embellished with seven different types of leaves, the walls became lighter, brighter, and more animated.

The middle portion of the photo shows three different sizes of ready-made canvases stretched over wooden frames. I glue gunned leaves directly to the untreated canvas surface; with time, the leaves have cracked and flaked. It's better to protect your leaf work under glass or plastic; the four large rectangular leaf pictures are much more durable.

BEFORE YOU START HOT GLUING LEAVES, CONSIDER THAT THEY ARE NOT ONLY THE MOST FRAGILE MEDIUM YOU CAN WORK WITH, BUT THEY ARE ALSO HELL TO KEEP CLEAN AND WHOLE. I don't like the look or feel of shellac on leaves (or any natural element), so I limit my leaf glue gunning to projects that I can protect under glass or acrylic. In my new library/guest room, I needed several bold hanging elements to disguise the room's cold gray stone walls. I couldn't find any four-foot-tall picture frames that were affordable. As I needed six of them and wanted them matching, I thought my only solution was to have them made, to the tune of a thousand dollars. Design dilemma! But like so many other times in my glue-gunning career, the answer was sitting in my local craft shop. For thirteen dollars apiece, I bought six poster frames with slim metal sides and clear acrylic fronts. Lightweight and easy to work on, they were the perfect solution.

Before you start gluing, divide your types of leaves into separate piles. (Work in a room without a draft because dried leaves can blow around.) Decide on the general shape of your motif. On a piece of white (or tan or beige) mat paper cut to the exact size of the frame (or on the ready-made oval or square canvas that comes with your frame), use a graphite pencil to outline the placement of your leaves. After your design is drawn on the canvas, paper, or wall, start your leaf work on the outer edge, not the center. The outside borders are the most difficult; Filling in the center is the most fun. Save the best for last. Keep it simple: Circles, squares, ovals, rectangles, or paisley shapes will pack more visual clout than a complicated design.

Set the temperature of your glue gun to "Regular" (low) and use the slim, needle-nosed nozzle with the slanted tip or the wide wedge to apply a thin amount of hot glue under each leaf. Avoid bending leaves when you attach them to the host surface because they will chip and break. Try to glue rapidly and pat the leaves in place quickly. Remember that the most beautiful pictures include white space around each leaf to add contrast and air.

Here are four different sizes of ready-made oval canvases. They are all three quarters of an inch thick, with canvas stretched over wooden bases and then attached on the sides with a staple gun.

TIP ONE: Before you adhere your leaves to matte paper, measure the spaces between groups of leaves to ensure that they are equal and even. Lay them all in place, and adjust their positions before you start gluing, then use a pencil to mark the spot where each leaf should be attached. Do not work in a drafty room—dried leaves flutter away!

TIP TWO: Draw your design directly on the host surface. Use pencil to trace the places where you will line up your specimens. When you have finished gluing, use an eraser to get rid of pencil marks.

TIP THREE: On a small frame, use smaller leaves around the edges, and larger ones in the middle. I ran out of tiny leaves this winter, so I cut crabapple leaves into smaller pieces to compensate. As leaves are brittle and fragile, they are not as maneuverable as shells, or pinecones. They will adhere more evenly if you apply the glue directly to the canvas.

REMOVING HOT GLUE THREADS AND FILAMENTS FROM LEAVES IS A DELICATE PROCESS. Try blowing them off with a hair dryer set on "low." You can also banish them by carefully whisking back and forth with a soft natural-hair makeup brush. Once your leaf pictures are safely covered in their frames, they will not budge or need cleaning.

Working with pinecones, acorns, thistles, and wheat shafts is another matter. Just as with shells, you can construct "pictures" (in frames but with no glass); they can also look gorgeous applied directly to walls and ceilings. As pinecones are brittle, delicate, and uneven, make sure to use your slim, slanted nozzle to apply hot glue on at least seven different "petals" to ensure a lasting bond. Acorns are slippery; after a month or two, an acorn seed might detach from its "hat," so hot glue the seed and the hat together before you adhere them to a wall or ceiling. Finally, lightweight dried weeds, seeds, small branches, and thistles will stay put forever, but they attract dust and lint. Even if you clean them every month by blowing them with a powerful hair dryer, they're continual magnets for anything flying through the air. A pineconed wall might be a thing of beauty, but spic-and-span it isn't. Neatniks, beware!

TIP ONE: To give your glue-gunned murals a sense of order and neatness, draw the shapes you will be filling with pinecones directly on the walls. The fifty-odd pinecone and acorn oval-shaped medallions glued on all four walls of my guest bedroom started out like this.

TIP TWO: When filling large shapes like this oval, it helps to start by gluing elements to the outside periphery first, then work in, creating concentric rows. Change your rustic materials every three rows or so for a more contrasted look.

TIP THREE: After you've gathered and dried several hundred specimens, begin your leaf picture projects by separating the leaves into piles according to type, size, and color.

1

2

3

Doing a makeover on a ho-hum cardboard container is one of the quickest, most satisfying ways to create a gift. This round, flat cylinder was transformed into a jewelry box fit for a fashionista in about twenty minutes. I used three yards of navy and white striped ribbon and eight feathers. I adhered ribbon to the top and the bottom of the lower part of the box and repeated the process on the lid, adding several strips of ribbon across the diameter. Each loop of the bow was applied individually. Once the bow looked pert and full, I glued six black feathers in between the loops by placing a generous glob of hot glue on the tip of the spine. This is not a box that can take a lot of wear and tear, but it will look super sitting on top of a dressing table or chest of drawers.

I started giving glue-gunned presents after one too many dinner guests left my house toting one of my handmade, embroidery-laden throw pillows. I had given them all away, of course, but I realized that making hot-glued gifts for birthdays, weddings, housewarmings, Christmas, and Mother's and Father's Day would be a way of keeping my decor at home while pleasing all those friends who wanted a piece of the action.

For Christmas last year, I bought twenty silk-covered sixteen-inch square pillows. Solid white and finished with a pretty one-inch-deep self-fringe, they were the perfect decorative foil for brightly colored embroidered embellishments (see chapter 2 for directions). Even better, they were the perfect gifts to ship to family and friends in Europe and California because they were post-office friendly—light as a feather and squeezable into almost any size box.

IF YOU MAKE GIFTS FOR FRIENDS, STICK WITH ITEMS THEY CAN USE, NOT TCHOTCHKES THAT CLUTTER UP CABINETS AND CLOSETS. One-of-a-kind small picture frames always come in handy—so do framed mirrors, placemats, and napkins, cachepots, tissue box covers, storage boxes, and agendas. The trick is to give made-to-order items: Use trims and embroidered motifs that match, or contrast favorably with your friends' and family's rooms. A picture frame designed for the top of your sister's bedroom dresser, for example, should reflect the color of her bedspread or curtains or rug. Ditto for tissue box covers; the colors of the passementerie or ribbon trim should reflect the color of the towels, tiles, or shower curtain in the particular bathroom.

No matter what item you are glue gunning, consider how much use it will get. A glue-gunned eyeglass case is not a good idea. All that handling and rattling around in a tote bag is not going to improve the appearance of a case covered in silk embroidery or grosgrain ribbon trim. Glue-gunned wallets, key holders, checkbook covers, and coin purses are also impractical gift ideas. Stick with presents that stay still on a shelf, table, or wall.

The quickest glue-gunned gift you can whip up is a small picture or mirror frame. Any frame under one and a half inches wide won't provide enough room for you to work with, so choose wider ones. You can find wooden frames everywhere, from flea markets to yard sales to discount stores, for less than five dollars. If your frames are varnished and you are not going to repaint them, sandpaper all gluable surfaces to assure a strong glue bond. Remove the glass from the frame before you start working, as glass can crack if it comes into contact with hot glue.

You can find new and old picture frames anywhere, from yard sales to fine department stores, but my favorite gift frames come from Target, Ikea, Kmart, and Wal-Mart. For as little as $2.99, you can work on a new frame without nicks, cracks, or chipped glass.

(above) To rig up this small frame, I first lined the inside frame border with shiny gold ribbon. Next, I made fluttery gold bows and glued them down at each inside corner. I glued down four pieces of red acrylic macramé cords, leaving an extra inch at each outside corner. Finally, I unraveled each of the eight red cord ends to make fringed tassels that extended beyond the corners. Total gluing time: one hour. Total cost: four dollars.

(above) This large frame was transformed in about twenty minutes, thanks to four feet of pale blue elastic trim and eight "leatherette" camellias that I bought at a discount store. To add a bit of further silliness, I glued three small loops of blue elastic to each corner.

(left and above) This handsome mirror is the perfect canvas for glue-gun designing. The wood is unfinished and rough, which makes for a strong hot-glue bond, and the three-and-a-half-inch width allows room for lots of trim action. I started by gluing one-and-five-eighths-inch white grosgrain ribbon in the middle of all sides. I added eight borders of yellow and black woven trim. As the ends unraveled severely each time I cut the trim, I used it to my advantage by unraveling it even more to create a "fringe" finish. Finally, the small black felt squares glued in the four corners hide some substandard scissors work on the grosgrain ribbon edges.

I FOUND THIS SIMPLE, MODERN WOODEN KLEENEX BOX COVER IN THE BACK OF A BATHROOM CUPBOARD, WHERE IT HAD LANGUISHED FOR ABOUT TEN YEARS. A bit faded and scuffed, the box's nice clean lines came right back into focus after I sprayed it with a light coat of black matte acrylic paint. After lightly sanding the areas to be glue gunned, I applied strips of white grosgrain ribbon on five sides, including the top. I then glued a narrower blue cotton ribbon over the white ribbon, leaving white showing on both sides. Finally, because some of the corner work looked a little fuzzy, I hot glued black felt squares to prevent further fraying.

A Kleenex box is a welcome gift for friends who like decorated bathrooms. Be sure to find out their color scheme before you start up this project.

(left) The bedecked Kleenex box looks spiffy in my guest bathroom. The blue, black, and white color scheme matches the towels and tiles. Even the white, cotton muslin curtains are trimmed with black and blue elastic.

STYLE NOTE: When you glue gun decorative accessories, "cute," frilly, and fussy designs should be avoided. Bathrooms are places for soothing and relaxing activities. Complicated details and motifs look and feel overwhelming in a well thoughtout bathroom. No more than three colors, please!

A CROWD-PLEASING GIFT THAT'S FUN TO CONCOCT IS A DECORATED CACHEPOT TO HIDE BANAL FLOWERPOTS. I found a square cachepot with wooden handles at my local supermarket. In galvanized tin, about ten inches high by ten inches wide at the top, it was the perfect size to hold houseplants. Unlike other glue-gun-friendly metals, galvanized tin has a slightly oily finish that will repel hot glue. You must rub all surfaces thoroughly with rubbing alcohol before you start.

I'm not a fan of fake flowers, but I made an exception for this cachepot, which I was making for Easter. I wanted to fill the pot with a white daisy plant, and I thought it would look more festive if I hot glued daisies to all four sides. I went to a large craft emporium that specializes in fake flowers, carrying a mind-numbing selection of silk and plastic blooms. There among the fake delphiniums, magnolias, and bluebells, I found sixteen perky Doris Day–like white daisies with fuzzy yellow centers. I covered each side of the pot with four daisies, so that they overlapped each other. Once the flowers were in place, I added inch-high loops of grosgrain ribbon to camouflage the top of the tin rim. The finished product looked like a fluffy floral poodle—and it looked even better filled with equally fluffy real daisies.

Craft shops are also super sources for cardboard and wooden boxes. In porous cardboard and balsa wood, these boxes are excellent surfaces on which to glue. Whether rectangular, round, or heart- or star-shaped, a box to hold jewelry, keys, coins, paperclips, pens and pencils, or makeup is a gift almost everyone can put into service. I like the tan and sand colors of the cardboard and balsa wood, so I glue trim directly over them, but you can also spray paint them before you start embellishing.

Holiday-themed boxes are great glue-gun craft projects. My next book will have plenty of holiday glue-gunning ideas, so stay tuned!

(above) Even a utilitarian galvanized tin cachepot can be the beginning of a mighty pretty decorative gift. I found this one at my local supermarket for about three dollars.

(opposite) After gluing the daisies in place, I added a dozen or so loops of lime green grosgrain ribbon to hide the metal sides and rim not covered by the daisy petals.

(next page) For the last page of this book, the easiest glue gun decor project of all: a place card–laden mirror. Even pizza and take-out meals become more festive when you place a personalized card at each guest's seat. You can use pieces of stationery, typing paper, cardboard, mat board, or Post-it notes. Just about any paper will do. After each meal, I collect the place cards and glue gun them to the mirror over the dining room fireplace. A dab of hot glue will not damage or break the mirror, nor mar the mirror's wooden frame. I started out affixing place cards around the inside of the mirror, and then proceeded to the molding and wall behind it. Caution: Hot gluing on older stucco walls will take off paint and plaster.